SOMEONE YOU LOVE IS OBSESSED WITH FOOD:

What You Need to Know About Eating Disorders

About the authors:

The authors are clinical psychologists who specialize in treating those with eating disorders. They have worked in the eating disorder field for many years. Linda Riebel, Ph.D., is the author of the book, *Understanding Eating Disorders: A Guide for Health Care Professionals*. She also has written many articles published in journals such as *Psychotherapy, Journal of Humanistic Psychology, Transactional Analysis Journal,* and *Small Group Behavior*. Jane Kaplan, Ph.D., is editor of the book, *A Woman's Conflict: the Special Relationship Between Women and Food*. She has explored parents' and children's problems with food and has written articles for *Working Mother Magazine* and *Pediatrics for Parents*.

SOMEONE YOU LOVE IS OBSESSED WITH FOOD:

What You Need to Know About Eating Disorders

Linda Riebel, Ph.D. and Jane Kaplan, Ph.D.

 HAZELDEN®

First published April 1989

ISBN: 0-89486-582-X

Library of Congress Catalog Card Number: 88-83559

Printed in the United States of America.

Editor's Note:
Hazelden Educational Materials offers a variety of information on chemical dependency and related areas. Our publica-
tions do not necessarily represent Hazelden or its programs,
nor do they officially speak for any Twelve Step organization.

The following publisher has generously granted permission
to reprint material from a copyrighted work: Reprinted with
permission of Bobbs-Merrill Co., an imprint of Macmillan Publishing Company, from FEEDING THE HUNGRY HEART by
Geneen Roth. Copyright © 1984 by Geneen Roth.

To my very special brother, Frank Riebel
— L. R.

To my children, Teddy and Abby
— J. R. K.

Contents

Preface

Eating problems are unfortunately very common in this time of fashionable thinness and exaggerated expectations for women and men. Primarily psychological in origin, they can also have medical and social consequences that concern the food-obsessed person—and those who care about him or her. This book is designed to teach you how to support and relate to a person with an eating problem.

Since the great majority of eating disordered persons are female, we have more often referred to the patient throughout this book as "she." Nevertheless, we have tried to give fair attention to men and boys who have eating disorders, by presenting a number of case histories of men and by dealing with the special concerns of men and boys in Chapter Fourteen.

It is a pleasure to acknowledge the help and support of our many friends and colleagues whose contributions, both direct and indirect, made this book possible. Avis Rumney and Ronna Kabatznick were instrumental in making it complete and thorough. Erica Goode and Marilyn Crim kindly reviewed the medical chapter. Laurel Mellin gave valuable help with the section on children and teenagers. Jacques Rutzky offered valuable input on alcohol abuse and treatment.

Reading the manuscript and offering much constructive advice were Carlos Gris, Hetty Jardine, Philip Cushman, Roxanne Head, Elizabeth Ratcliff, Ginny Conger, Kay Debs, and Olga Grinstead. Violet Riebel, Marina Baroff, Kate Kaplan, Nori Burk, Cheryl Kruater, and Andrew Condey were also supportive.

1

Jeannie Pinault helped make the book readable and "user friendly." We also wish to thank Kerry Finn and Jeff Petersen at Hazelden.

All cases described are composites of many individual patients. Identifying factors have been changed to preserve the privacy of actual people we have treated.

CHAPTER 1

The Pudge and the Freshman Ton: A Therapist Recalls Her Struggle with Food

by Linda Riebel

When a new client comes into my office, she may be wary, imagining I am a book expert who offers facts and disapproval. Sometimes I ease these fears by telling her about my own struggle with eating, which took place many years ago.

As a youngster, I played ball, climbed trees, and generally burned up all the cookies and cakes I ate. Then in fourth grade, a crush on a classmate made me aware of my body. I felt imperfect, on trial. One night in bed I felt so urgently the need to do something *right now* that I decided to exercise then and there. Pedaling my legs, tossing the bedclothes awry, I prayed that this would fix me so I would be liked.

At thirteen I went away to an elegant summer school. The other girls weren't interested in climbing trees or dreaming up ideas for books that would make them famous. They were dressing up for the dances. Quickly I discovered that I, too, wanted to be pretty and get boys' attention. Then, as now, one had to be slim. Trying to look right, I would run up and down the dormitory steps a dozen, two dozen, five dozen times. Fat fear gives you stamina!

Back in my hometown high school, the popular girls were set apart, as if by caste lines, from the others. I marveled at how the "in" girls did it. Was it clothes? Was it smiling? I never did find out. A born wallflower, I yearned for dates but shrank from the few boys who approached. Once I even hid when one came calling with a birthday present.

For some reason, however, I had the gall to enter the "Miss Arlington" contest the summer after I graduated. Amazingly, I was advanced to the semifinals. This minor success in the Cool Appearance Sweepstakes was a tremendous boost. Imagine actually being in a pageant, answering questions into a microphone, meeting a television celebrity! I could dream about riding in the Fourth of July parade, waving proudly to all the people who had been aloof. Years later I was embarrassed by the whole shallow spectacle, but when I was an insecure teenager, validation of my looks was something I craved. It would mean I was Neat, I was Okay. People would look and sigh and envy. Envy would mean I was a good person.

Two weeks after my seventeenth birthday, I went off to college at Wellesley, which is full of bright girls (we were called "girls" then). Here studying was not only hard, it was frightening. Those alien things, C's and D's, would appear on my papers. I was terrified, and studied even harder, guilty over taking the shortest break, awash in anxiety, losing my bearings altogether.

According to Wellesley tradition, by the end of the first year, each entering class of four hundred students would collectively gain at least two thousand pounds. This was the Freshman Ton. We laughed about it and ate. I gained more than my share.

College is a twenty-four-hour-a-day job. There are always more books to read, more footnotes to add. I rediscovered woman's best friend, food. Waking up to each day guaranteed to bring new anxieties, so I would go down to the kitchen, where the staff had cooked eggs, bacon, pancakes, hot cereal, toast, all paid for in room and board. All I had to do was load my tray.

Then, after a hard morning of exposure to the vastness of the universe and my own ignorance, lunch was a welcome relief. The trek back to the dorm was brightened by the prospect of food at the end of it. Did you know that studying makes you crave starch? Down with chemical formulae, diplomatic history, theories of philosophy, and terror. A good, solid dish of spaghetti was definite, palpable, seeming to whisper, *This is for me.* Dinner was the same, an island of balm in a sea of worry. A lot of us made food our friend, and overeating raised not a stigma but the rueful laugh of recognition. We were putting on the Freshman Ton.

"Only Fourteen Hours Till Breakfast"

Three meals a day are not enough for the truly anxious. I remember pushing my chair back from dinner and thinking, *Only fourteen hours till breakfast.* With family, pets, familiar landmarks, and activities all gone, only food remained as a sign of stability.

Then I discovered chewing gum. This was cheap, lightweight, less fattening than ice cream, and longer lasting. I developed a partiality for boxes of little, square Chiclets covered in colors like candy. I devoured loads of them as I studied nervously in my upper bunk. I was a chain-chewer. Sometimes I would miss the wastebasket, and little gobs of calcified fear would be stuck to the walls and floor until I got down to clean them up.

Even so, I gained weight. Every day I would climb on the scales, fearing what the oracle would say.

- *Gained a pound, you sinner! Why didn't you stay at the library?*
- *Hah, hah, all that dieting didn't help.*

Then the rationalizations would set in.

- *That really wasn't that big a breakfast. Besides, I dieted last night. That was a kind of belated Tuesday meal, so really I'm even for today and yesterday.*
- *Gee, I wish I hadn't had that brownie—the apple at four o'clock was supposed to be my whole snack.*

At this point I would picture the two offending snacks, and try to merge them visually onto one plate.

- *Yes, that's better. One plate of food isn't so bad. I will just call that my dinner and for sure I'll skip dinner tonight.*

These mental somersaults did no good whatsoever. By 6:00 P.M., after a struggle, I would bolt downstairs for dear life and find a place at the table.

- *Really,* I would tell myself, *I needed the break. I'll study better when I go back up. I'll just have a few of these beans... .*

How strange! The hand does not listen to vows or commands. The hand reaches out to the meat and potatoes, bringing back repeat servings, ignoring the brain's frantic monologues. Which was me, the hand-mouth team or the voice?

Underneath it all was a scared seventeen-year-old coping with overwork, competition, loneliness, fear—and men. Dating was a weird business in the mid-1960s. From Monday to Friday, 1,700 girls (we became women around 1966) in jeans, with no makeup, plowed into books, no men in sight. On Friday afternoon, the dorms hummed with electric shavers and hairdryers. We still used girdles then, those woven rubber fat compactors meant to squash the blubber below the waist. After dinner on Friday the transformed butterflies would emerge for evening dates.

In 1965 it was still an issue whether "nice" girls had sex or not. Our upbringing had taught fear and suspicion about boys. The double standard meant hypocrisy, dares, dreading one's own natural impulses, using each other, and pretending to be innocent. Admiration from men was delicious, and kissing all very pleasant—but the rest—ugh! I could hardly believe people my age were—you know, *doing it.*

It wasn't long before I had to take a stand. In my sophomore year, my boyfriend sweetly but insistently pressed for sex. I didn't really know what "it" involved. A friend, diagnosing my state of ignorance (Gee, food really was the only thing I knew anything about!) gave me a book explaining sex to young women. This was a mistake. It must have been a reprint of something written in 1905. Its description of the male's excitation was horrifying: he drools, his eyes glaze over, his nose begins to run (I'm not kidding, this was in the book). ... This terrified me and I gave up the young man.

So my dates continued to draw to a close at the front door with a polite, frozen smile. Eating was still good, clean fun though. Once, nervous in front of my date and two other couples, I consumed two gigantic helpings of peppermint ice cream. I vaguely sensed that this was not right. There seemed something a little strange about continuing to eat long after everyone else had stopped.

Others were more successful—or so I thought. One year a girl in my dorm was skeletally thin. I didn't know her name, but I could see her wraith-like form scuttling down the halls. I was amazed and jealous. She brought diet salad dressing to the dinner table, because salad was all she would eat and the dorm's oil and vinegar was "too fattening." I wished I had her willpower. Then one day she disappeared. Months later we learned she had died.

I kept eating, and even workouts on the rowing and fencing teams didn't keep my weight down. One day I thought of a solution. Locking myself in the bathroom, I tried to induce vomiting. But somehow my system didn't want to go into reverse.

To the person who is (or feels) fat, nothing is more agonizing than to have a thin, *blithe* friend. A few girls in the dorm could actually sit at the table and talk about something other than food. Ann talked about music, but all I noticed was how she could put her knees together and you could see space between her thighs. Joan murmured one spring, "Gee, if I'd only dieted in March I could wear a bikini now." I could have killed her. Didn't she know she already looked like a model? How could she not be happy? If only I could weigh 110 pounds, all my problems would disappear. This belief led me into a vicious circle: Worry about weight led to self-hate (or sprang from it), and food was the only consolation. This created fat, which led to even more worry about weight. I couldn't escape!

To me, men were the Real People, the ones I was supposed to please and impress. The male-dominance mystique meant I was born inferior, but maybe I could overcome this primal defect through brilliance. Just let me catch your attention with my stunning—er, slightly rounded looks, and then I'll pour out all the brilliant theories I've had since yesterday. I ran away from that charming first boyfriend and took up with a shadier character, who was all I thought I deserved. He called me "the pudge," crystallizing the dread that body image is, after all, the main element of identity.

Miraculously, I graduated on time, and not even at the bottom of my class. Back in my hometown, I met a wonderful guy who showed me what "It" was all about, so I didn't feel weird and left out anymore. I never knew you could have so much fun without eating!

"They'll Have to Love Me as I Am ..."

At twenty-two I spent a year in Europe. With no formal assignments, no financial worries, and all of European art to explore, I was at last happy. There was another blessing. A culture less obsessed with slimness showed me where the real problem lay. One day, waiting for my Florentine boyfriend to pick me up, I was struck as if by lightning. *All this dieting is to please other people! Well, hang it! They'll have to love me as I am, or not at all.* Suddenly the entire layer of guilt and fear vanished. I could please myself!

My eating habits didn't change instantly, so it took several years to slim down to pre-college weight. By age twenty-seven, I realized I was normal—not a fat person momentarily thin, a pudge precariously poised on a ledge between peaks of fat, but a permanently thin person who could be trusted to eat normally, except for occasional minor slips in times of stress. Now, years later, I look back on what I learned.

- Happiness is not a magic number on a scale. Happiness (for me) came first, and normal appetite after.
- Men do love women with imperfect bodies. I hadn't seen this before, because I believed imperfect people don't get loved.
- Impossible goals backfire. An oath sworn to be in *total control* tomorrow may give momentary confidence, but it's an illusion. The higher the standard one sets, the easier it is to fall short and tumble into a binge as punishment.
- Trying to understand the "meaning" of a lapse almost always made things worse as long as I was trying to look perfect. Either I would invent a pathetic rationalization, or I would come to a self-blaming conclusion that I deserved to fail. Neither helped.
- Most importantly, I learned that to reach for food is to reach for something normal: consolation, protection, defiance, pleasure. The ultimate solution to an eating disorder is to learn what you want, how to get it (or to live without getting it), and how to live with the interim period of uncertainty.

CHAPTER 2

Not My Daughter!

You may be wondering whether your child, roommate, friend, partner, or spouse has one of those eating disorders you have heard so much about. She struggles with her weight, talking constantly about food, figures, and diets. She seems to hate herself and puts off making decisions and getting on with life. An obsession with fat and food has replaced her optimism and ambition. You wonder if below the surface there are more serious worries.

Or perhaps a person you care about has just told you she is bulimic. Where did she get this idea—from a magazine, a friend, or a qualified professional? The sensationalized stories in the media? You may wonder, *What did I do wrong? What shall I do now? Could she die of this?*

You want impartial advice. Discussing the issue with family and friends might embarrass your loved one. The family doctor is competent, but often too busy to talk at length, and besides, he or she may not be an expert on eating disorders. What to do?

We have met and talked with many worried relatives and friends in our years of treating patients with eating disorders. These relatives and friends call us to ask what they can do. This book is intended to help you begin a constructive, new relationship with a person who has an eating disorder: anorexia, bulimia, or compulsive eating. It is not intended as a substitute for professional treatment, or to take the place of Twelve Step programs like Overeaters Anonymous, O-Anon, and Al-Anon, but

13

rather to supplement them. Psychotherapy and Twelve Step programs can be powerful allies to help friends and families of people with eating disorders.

> *Amy is five feet, eight inches and weighs ninety pounds — ninety and a half, to be exact. Her problem began shortly before her honeymoon in Hawaii. Her anxious husband, Howard, says he thought it was because she wanted to look good in a bathing suit. When the starving didn't stop after she lost weight, Howard got scared. He forced her into treatment, where she has been for three months without any improvement that he can see. Now he is afraid he may have done more harm than good by coercing her.*

> *Lana, the mother of one of our severely bulimic clients called from out of town, mystified about her daughter's disorder and treatment. Lana had read somewhere that mothers cause bulimia in their daughters. She is worried about her child and her possible role in creating the disorder.*

> *A young wife named Zoe called, "just wondering" about her husband's compulsive refrigerator raiding. She says she has to keep party refreshments in her neighbor's freezer or they will disappear before guests arrive. She supposes she is failing him in some way.*

What's the Problem?

Attention to food and eating can be quite natural. Most people have a normal, healthy interest in tasty foods and in being nourished regularly. But many people sometimes become preoccupied with food. Most teenagers, as their bodies change, find diet is one factor they can experiment with. And it is natural for a new mother, after giving birth, to try to restore her body to its familiar dimensions.

Many people are creating new food habits in light of recent discoveries about diet's relationship to heart disease, cancer, and longevity. And for many of us, diet certainly is a time-honored topic of conversation! Interest in food and eating is not a cause for concern if it only takes the form of conversation, if the physical health is robust, and if other aspects of the person's life (such as work, relationships, and self-esteem) are satisfactory.

Yet concern with eating can go too far. An actual, diagnosable eating disorder is more than just a temporary fascination with food and weight control. An eating disorder is a habitual practice of compulsive eating, eating and throwing up, overusing laxatives, or eating so little that the weight drops dangerously. There are rare medical reasons for a person to overeat or refuse food. But if no medical cause is found, the diagnosis of eating disorder may be made.

Actual eating disorders start in the mind. This does not mean that the person you care about is crazy. It means she has attached inappropriate meanings to the business of nourishment, and these inappropriate meanings distort her perceptions. Hilde Bruch, who wrote the first and foremost books on eating disorders, called them "a misuse of the eating function to solve problems of living."[1] This is the best definition we know.

How can a person use eating—or not eating—to "solve problems of living"? Here is an example.

> *Lisa is thirteen. Every afternoon she comes home from school and stuffs herself with cookies, cake, and any other sweet thing she can find, and then vomits them away. She has been doing this since her father moved out and her mother became preoccupied with wresting an acceptable financial settlement from him. Six months after the separation, Lisa's mother notices that her once-cheerful daughter has become pale, withdrawn, and has lost interest in her scouting group and her hiking club.*

When a person has an eating disorder, she has chosen to use food to address emotional problems—loneliness, grief, anger, fear, or planning a future. With her gradually ballooning or wasting body, with her rituals and obsessions, she may be sending her family and friends a message:

- "Notice me."
- "I defy your ideas of beauty."
- "I hate myself."
- "Set firmer rules."
- "If I stay messed up, maybe Mom and Dad won't fight so much."
- "If I'm thin, then will you love me?"
- "If I'm fat, then will you stop worrying that I may leave you for another man?"
- "I don't deserve to be happy."
- "I'm scared of growing up."
- "I'd rather die than do things your way."
- "I can't cope."
- "I have no idea what I'm feeling."

There are as many messages as there are people with eating disorders. Living up to society's expectations, suppressing anger or other feelings, and coping with low self-esteem and psychological pain are commonly involved. After talking to a therapist, Lisa's mother knows now that her teenager is signaling her. The message is, *Don't you go away too! I need you!*

Kate's Journey

Let's meet one of our eating disordered patients in depth, someone we'll call Kate. As we follow Kate's story, we'll meet her again and again as we trace the root of her problem, how it affected the people who loved her, how she came to get help, and how it all turned out.

This story began as a question in the mind of a friend, Joy, who first met Kate while they were in college together. Joy liked Kate's attentiveness, the interest she showed in others, her engaging conversation, and skill in skating. A few years later they met again and their friendship renewed. They decided to share an apartment. After a month or two Joy began to notice a few things including missing food, and the amount of time Kate spent in the bathroom. Kate wouldn't go out to social events with Joy, and she avoided shared meals. She evaded certain obligations with guilty apologies, and her interest in her favorite sport fluctuated erratically. Though they seemed close in many ways, Kate shrugged off Joy's concerned questions. Her denial of any problem seemed so sincere that Joy let it slide. Yet Kate began to look pale, and she stayed in her room a lot. Joy asked herself what was going on. How could things be so different now for someone Joy used to think she understood?

CHAPTER 3

A Glimpse Into Another World

Eating is so simple. Why can't my partner/daughter/friend use food normally? This question echoes in the minds of countless people across the country.

People without eating problems are mystified by the sufferer's inability to stop unhealthy behaviors she may no longer even want. To them, her problem may even seem to be exaggerated. But food obsession is not trivial or self-indulgent. Far from being frivolous, the food-obsessed person is often guilt-ridden, driven, and unhappy.

If good advice and common sense were as easy to swallow as ice cream, the person you are worried about could be cured of an eating disorder in an instant. A simple instruction would be enough: "If you're too skinny, start eating. If you're too fat, diet and exercise. If you're throwing up to dispose of mega-snacks, stop it." Unfortunately, people are not this logical. If we were, not many of us would smoke, gamble, drink, or abuse other drugs. The person with the problem has almost certainly tried this logic already, and it hasn't worked.

Let us help you try to see the world from the eyes of a person with an eating disorder. She probably does not perceive the world as a comfortable place, and it is especially uncomfortable inside her mind. Her inner conflicts may feel like intruders who mischievously take over and get her into trouble. In one corner is an impulse that may seem like a sort of demon that must be forever chained and guarded or it will take over. In the other corner is a critic who offers no help in controlling the beast, but is always ready to blame when it escapes.

For the person obsessed with food, self-respect depends on how "good" she has been today, or this week, or this month (how successful she has been in restraining her eating). With one little slip her self-esteem slides into an abyss. There, her despair can only be relieved by the one consolation she knows: food.

Imagine how life would feel if you did not believe the world would accept you unless you were perfect—physically, mentally, and in every other way.

Imagine how you would feel about your family and friends if you believed you did not deserve to get anything you really wanted.

Imagine the pressure you would feel if your first law was to control your emotions at all times.

If you can picture these states of mind, you can begin to relate to the internal battle going on inside your loved one, even if you can't see it on the surface.

Masking Inner Conflicts

One can hide many personal conflicts behind food abuse. *Anger* is a prime example. In some families and cultures, anger is forbidden. A child born into this family or culture learns to suppress anger. Stuffing food down one's throat is a powerful way to stuff down anger, or any other feeling, since you can't speak or cry with your mouth full. Self-hate can result from stuffing one's emotions in this way, but for some people it is safer than feeling anger at others.

Assertiveness is another important issue that may be hidden behind unhealthy eating. Many food-obsessed people feel unworthy to ask directly for what they want. Instead, they use indirect means: being nice, looking hopeful, hinting, and earning it three times over. Sometimes they become caregivers, offering to others the very things they need themselves. Since *pleasing people* is so important to them, they have developed masks of apparent confidence behind which can lie problems hidden for years, from friends, relatives, and even themselves.

When people feel they can never do enough to redeem themselves in the eyes of a critical, hostile world, they become people-pleasers. For example, some people with eating disorders choose careers such as nursing or teaching in which they are rewarded for functioning in a helping or pleasing role.

Body image plays a part in the fasting-overeating cycle. If I feel that the solution to misery lies in thinness, I will orient my life toward achieving thinness, putting off everything else until I am slim enough. Most of the eating disordered clients we have seen feel their bodies are unattractive, ugly, uncontrollable—their enemies. This makes normal eating difficult: why bother to take good care of something you hate?

Like money, food is a currency pressed into service for bad as well as for good. For instance, a person may use eating for not only nutrition but also to pass the time, to punish oneself or others, to procrastinate, or to keep people away.

Food obsession may involve not only self-hate but also loss of control, loss of body awareness, above-average spending on food or diet-related items, and dread of holidays or other special occasions. Sadly, it also can divert energy and talent. After examining her feelings in therapy for some time, Helen exclaimed one day, "Just think! Now that I'm overcoming this obsession, I can start working toward my bachelor's degree again!" Others have regained energy for sports, classes, relationships, and creativity.

Control is a central theme for people with eating disorders. It is unthinkable to them to relax control over their thoughts, feelings, words, or actions. The common fear is that if control is relaxed, even for an instant, disaster will follow. The illusion is that peace of mind can be purchased with eternal vigilance. The cruel trick is that the food-obsessed person gets the vigilance without the peace of mind.

Advertisements, television shows, and movies reveal our imperfections. We are shown in full color how our thighs "should" look. Our own bathing suits leave us exposed for the world to see and (we dread) to judge. Since the media show almost no women with less-than-perfect bodies, the illusion is given that "if you don't look like this, you're nobody." To figure-obsessed women, the identity itself is precarious, dependent on success in dieting, forfeited at the least transgression.

But not all eating disordered people are obsessed with their figures. Some people began over- or undereating to cope with a loss, or during an illness, and then found they couldn't break the pattern.

Perfectionism is a characteristic of many bulimics and anorexics. They drive themselves to have excellent grades, the boss's approval, the wittiest conversations and, of course, the perfect figure. If they fall short of their expectations, they judge themselves harshly, shun praise, worry, and work too hard. This perfectionism is not usually the love of doing a good job, but a driven fear of rejection. Perfect behavior or performance seems to offer a route to some sort of acceptance. Unfortunately, the perfectionist almost never gives herself full marks for a good job, since she is imagining an even more perfect performance. So even success brings no praise or pleasure. It is as if the eating disordered person must be perfect, but cannot be happy.

But what is this perfectionism for? It may represent a hope that a perfect performance can be a substitute for herself, which she dislikes and distrusts. It's as if she says, "My schoolwork, my house, my mothering, my body are me. This is all of me."

Even if the desired praise results, it doesn't really soothe the anxiety. The hurting, invisible person within who *produces* the perfect performance remains hidden, feeling unseen and still insufficient. So, seeing no way out of this vicious circle, she tries even harder to be perfect.

> *Maureen constantly put herself down. Nothing she did was good enough in her eyes. Kevin, her husband of three years,*

was amazed and confounded. It was depressing to hear her berate herself day after day. He tried everything to lift her spirits. He praised, cajoled, kidded. But she continued to demand only the best from herself, becoming upset if anything "went wrong." She was also critical of Kevin, who was an easygoing man.

Even though Kevin thought she was beautiful, Maureen hated her body. After a party she would criticize every person there, including herself. Maureen binged and purged since she couldn't keep her weight down to model size any other way. She still felt fat and ugly. She spent a lot of energy hating her weak will.

When she finally realized that she was being too critical, she tried to change her thinking. What's wrong with me? *she wondered.* I have everything—a loving husband, a good job, a lovely apartment. *Then she berated herself for not being more contented.*

Maureen had spent so much of her life criticizing herself that it was a revelation to learn in recovery how much else there is to life. Some people with eating disorders must work hard in recovery to stop blaming themselves and accept life's satisfactions.

Relationships with other people, instead of being restorative and supportive, often feel draining to those with eating disorders. Those we have known are generally hungry for love and respect. They go out to meet the world from a position of high need and low self-esteem, convinced, *I'm not okay, and I must hide this dreadful secret—cover it up with perfectionism, or earn love by niceness and taking care of people's every wish.*

This is a disadvantageous position from which to meet other people. The eating disordered person, convinced the other person is better, suspects the other person thinks so too. She thinks the other person is busy judging her, and can just imagine what the other is saying. So she tries hard to please. But this hard work creates resentment—which must be hidden. She feels imprisoned and isolated.

The people in her world are cast as potential or actual critics:

- the person who must be placated;
- the person she is angry at (but doesn't dare confront);
- the enviable, successful one;
- the authority figure such as a teacher or a beautiful model she is supposed to look like;
- the friend who blithely takes up her time;
- the person she is supposed to be rescuing.

There are also men who are to be impressed, and men who are sexually threatening. There are very few people who are seen as nurturing and accepting, or less acceptable than the patient herself.

Her relationships with others are contaminated by her relationship with her body. It accompanies her like an unwelcome guest in every encounter with other people. She may feel that her body is not the one she intends to spend the rest of her life with: this is not her real body—so this meeting, this friendship, this connection or romance or opportunity, is not wholly real either. At best, it is a dress rehearsal for when she becomes thin and perfect.

How You Can Provide Support

As mentioned earlier, the way you think may not seem logical to the person with an eating disorder. In fact, it can intensify her feelings of being different and helpless to break the vicious circle of eating, guilt, and self-hate. The well-meant cries, "Eat!" or "Stop eating!" can drive her deeper into her problem.

Gillian, a recovered bulimic, explained the "rules" she had lived by during her teens and early twenties, when her problem was at its peak:

> *I'm not good enough, but I'm supposed to be perfect. So I must take care of others first. It helps if I get good grades, so I study very hard. If I let go of my tight control I'm convinced*

I'll melt or explode or maybe disappear; I especially can't show anger or aggression. I should be the best because, if not, I must be the worst.

To many people with eating disorders, this is how the world works, and it isn't an easy world to live in! Give your loved one credit for doing as well as she does with work or school while coping with all this. Your understanding can provide support while she explores and tries to resolve hidden problems. In later sections, we will suggest ways to express your understanding and concern.

For many eating disordered people, inner conflicts are constantly raging.

- They feel worthless but have high expectations for themselves.
- They try to fulfill the social roles of both female and male.
- Their hunger for affection battles the habit of appeasing and taking care of others.
- They treat the body as an ugly, disobedient servant, robbing themselves of a source of the pleasure and consolation they sorely need.
- They desire to be attractive but fear the vulnerability that mature sexuality requires.

To bulimics, life is

a series of nightmarish transitions from relative calm to revulsion and loathing; how tenuous and fragile is their capacity for control; how much effort they expend to maintain control for even a few hours; and how purging, for all its horrible effects, is all that stands between them and an anticipated loss of all self-worth. They accept the pain of purging rituals gladly, as the only remaining test of endurance they know they can pass.

To succeed in a world now requiring male toughness, their ability to starve and purge becomes the only remaining vestige of toughness to which they can point. Emotionally, physically, and socially enfeebled, they dread a future of dependence and mediocrity, but doubt their capability for anything else. If they fear growing up and facing the demands of adult life, it is not only because they do not know what to be, but also because they no longer have the energy reserves to "be" anything.[1]

We have many sayings in English that connect eating with anger, frustration, or other unpleasant emotions or events: eating crow, eating your heart out, ramming something down someone's throat, swallowing your pride — even cramming for an examination. An eating disorder is a sort of powerful and dangerous saying in action.

Little did Joy know that Kate's inner life was drastically different from what she presented to the world. Behind Kate's friendly, competent facade lay a scared, obsessed person who was convinced people would not really like her if they knew the real Kate. She had learned many ways to hide this true self. She was so good at it, in fact, that people even turned to her for advice, thinking that she "had it all together."

But sometimes Kate was so tired and lonely, tired of pleasing everyone and doing everything perfectly, that she would lock herself in her room with a bag of cookies and a gallon of ice cream. She would eat until she couldn't hold any more. It felt awful afterward, but while she was chewing and swallowing, all her troubles seemed to disappear.

But they reappeared, with a vengeance, as soon as Kate stopped eating. Agonies of self-hate would well up. I can't believe it! *she would cry to herself.* I broke my promise again! I'm such a wimp. If I can't do one simple thing, how do I expect to ever amount to anything? *At this point she would go to bed and cry herself to sleep, usually swearing to herself,* Tomorrow for sure I'll be good.

CHAPTER 4

Ways Eating Goes Wrong

In this chapter we will explain how people become preoccupied with food. We will also define the different eating disorders, explain how labels such as "bulimia" or "anorexia" must be approached with caution, and show you that eating disorders can be cured.

Why Food?

How does food get enlisted in a person's internal struggle? To someone who is healthy, the idea may seem alien. But some sources of eating problems are close at hand. First, we must all face food every day of our lives. Second, through the ages eating has been a source of pleasure, a way of expressing love for others, and an important part of socializing. For humans, food has always served other functions besides nourishment.

Eating disorders develop partly because food is such an all-purpose substance. It can be an anesthetic, friend, enemy, and hobby. To the healthy person, food serves three functions:

- it sustains life;
- it is a source of pleasure; and
- it is a social glue.

The most important rituals and passages through life—for example, weddings, bar mitzvahs, and graduations—are accompanied by food.

To the person with an eating conflict, food serves dozens of additional functions. Our clients told us that food serves as

- a consolation;
- a reward;
- an anesthetic;
- a procrastination device;
- a way to comply (accepting offered food);
- a punishment (*I don't deserve to feel good about myself*);
- a way of showing love;
- a means of expressing creativity;
- a diversion in times of boredom.

These uses of food don't, by themselves, indicate a disorder. It is only the *quantity* and *combinations* of such traits that create an illness. For instance, the healthy person may attach to food some of the meanings listed above, but not to an extent that creates a problem.

Using food as an all-purpose coping mechanism has a terrible drawback. In our culture extra weight may be severely punished with ridicule and discrimination. Thus, a person who relies on food as support may feel forced to "undo" its effects through dieting, purging, overexercising, or all three.

Ironically, even fat serves a role in an eating disorder. You might think fat, so hated in our culture, would be useless. But in each person's internal world, even problems or symptoms serve a function. That is, they keep us moving in a certain way, or keep us from having to face even worse problems or symptoms. The woman with a stomachache doesn't have to think about her shaky relations with her boss; the man obsessed with money doesn't have to feel the depth of his grief over a loss, and so on. Fat, like food itself, can play many roles. It can be a

- punishment (*I'm no good, and don't deserve to be thin*);
- delaying mechanism (*I'll have to wait until later to buy new clothes, get a new job, meet people, try out for a play...*);
- shield (*No one can see the real me*);

- defiance (*I refuse to be the way you say I should*);
- sign of loyalty (*I'm just like Mom*);
- warning (*Men, stay away*);
- friend (*I'm not alone*);
- sign of substantiality (*I believe thinness equals weakness*).

A woman may consciously want to be thin, but in her unconscious mind may wonder, *How will I keep men away if I'm thin?* We frequently hear clients reveal versions of this conflict. Unconscious motives drive them to the refrigerator to keep the hefty fat-shield in place while their conscious mind insists on trying to diet. That is why they feel so miserable—there is a civil war going on!

A person can physically abstain from alcohol or other drugs, or cigarettes, but never from food. This is a disheartening truth for a person who may wish she could just go cold turkey from her nemesis—but knows that as long as she lives she must face it every day.

A Short Course in Eating Behavior: Definitions

Problem behavior with food shows up in a great many ways. There are many possible combinations of restraint and excess in eating, and many ways a person can try to erase "mistakes."

Overeating can consist of

- nibbling all day ("grazing");
- consuming excessively large meals; or
- bingeing.

Technically, a *binge* occurs when a person eats a large quantity of food (for example, many full-sized meals) in a relatively short time. Some people, however, use the word "binge" to describe a smaller amount (an extra serving or even a single cookie) if they felt out of control at the time.

Purging is the practice of trying to escape the consequences of overeating by getting rid of food, either by vomiting or by using laxatives or diuretics (substances that facilitate bowel emptying or urination).

Restricting means eating less than the person needs, such as in severe dieting or anorexia. A person who restricts food intake by overriding her natural hunger signals feels she is demonstrating her willpower. Actually it only sets her up for her next overindulgence.

As she ignores her genuine hunger, a restricting, figure-conscious person may criticize herself for not living up to some mythical, dietetic ideal. She may feel disgusted or frightened, thinking she must purge or vow to go on a new diet. If this pattern becomes entrenched, the person can lose track of what it is to eat healthfully, what fullness feels like, or what her body really looks like, feels, and needs. Every advertisement or off-hand remark about thinness reminds her of the ideal image to which she may not conform. To people with low self-esteem, such criticism prompts redoubled efforts to be perfect.

A lifelong dieter describes how it feels to be constantly restricting:

> *I feel I have no natural control over my eating like others do. I feel if I'm not on a mechanical, go-by-the-book diet, then I would be unable to eat natural amounts to maintain my weight. I am obsessed with thoughts of food. Since I can't eat due to my diet, I read about dieting, figure out really low-cal, filling foods, keep a perfect record of my calories. I feel this is unnatural. No one else has a shadow hanging over their heads all day, affecting their every action, thought and interaction with others. A constant fear of losing control, and if I give in I will be at the mercy of a repulsive gorger, doomed to get fat because I would eat more calories than my body requires. Why can't I be normal, to eat and only think of food when my body needs it for physiological functioning, and then spend and live my life with other thoughts and actions totally unrelated to food? I feel like a prisoner.[1]*

Eating Disorders: Definitions

Now let us look at eating disorders—when problem *behavior* becomes an *illness*.

Bulimia involves eating large quantities of food in a relatively short time. Most bulimics use high-carbohydrate foods such as ice cream, cookies, and bread for their binges. Some maintain normal eating patterns apart from bingeing, while others can scarcely recall when they last ate normally. Many bingers further risk their health by purging to get rid of the effects of a binge (the full feeling and dread of gaining weight). Others never purge, but live with the discomfort of being overfull and the anxiety of being or becoming overweight.

The bulimic knows her behavior is abnormal but feels helpless to stop it. She may have tried many times to overcome her problem without telling anyone. Secrecy is an important and painful part of the problem for many bulimics.

> *The inside of a binge is deep and dark; it is a descent into a world in which every restriction you have placed on yourself is cut loose. The forbidden is obtainable. Nothing matters— not friends, not family, not lovers. Nothing matters but food. Lifting, chewing, swallowing—mechanical, frenzied acts, one following the other until a physical limit, usually nausea, is reached. Then comes the sought after numbness, the daze, the indifference to emotional pain. Like a good drug, food knocks out sensation.*[2]

There are other bulimic patterns. Some people force themselves to throw up after eating a normal-sized meal, or even after a snack. Some chew food and spit it out without swallowing. Since so many combinations of bingeing and purging behaviors exist, no chart or set of psychological definitions can cover all cases. Some people call themselves "bulimic" even if they overeat just a bit but feel out of control about it, or if they have induced vomiting even once. For our purposes, labeling your friend's problem is less important than making sure help is on the way.

Like bulimia, *anorexia nervosa* is a dangerous disorder. Anorexics reduce their food intake, usually saying they want to be thinner. But even when they have succeeded in becoming thin, anorexics continue to starve themselves, saying they still feel fat, or some part of their body is still fat.

The distortion of body image is so extreme that an anorexic may feel fat even while weighing well below normal. By definition, an anorexic, regardless of sex, is at least 15 percent below the normal weight for height. The female anorexic has missed her menstrual period for several months. Some anorexics keep their weight low by uninterrupted, rigid dieting; others intersperse a Spartan diet with binges and purges. Taken to extremes, self-imposed starvation can lead to medical dangers that require hospitalization. Some anorexics die.

According to one recovered anorexic who is now a therapist,

> *The anorexic is determined to maintain control in order to avoid experiencing the pain—the fear, the anger and the grief— of someone else's being in charge and denying her what she needs or wants. The anorexic will attempt to assert and maintain control of situations, particularly where they relate to food. The prospect of loss of control is very scary to the anorexic. Without control, she will experience that emptiness, that void, which feels threatening, cold, deathlike. By hoarding and saving food, she can control the presence (to her the existence) of food.*
>
> *While hungry and deliberately starving herself, she is determined to maintain control of her own food intake. Food becomes to her much more than a means of sustenance or an expression that she is in charge of her own life. It is also a symbol for love. It is something she can hang onto and keep with her—an anorexic frequently carries with her a squashed cookie or other morsel of food, wrapped in a paper napkin, crushed into the bottom of her bag. She may never eat the*

cookie, but its presence gives her a sense of security, like a blanket or a stuffed animal to a small child.[3]

Obesity is not an eating disorder as such. It's a state of carrying too much fat. And fat can come from more than one source. A person may have a genetic predisposition to be heavy, or a rare medical condition. Slight overeating and underexercising can, over decades, lead to gradual but substantial weight gain. But it is not easy to determine what is "too much fat." Heaviness is partly determined by genes, partly by eating habits, and partly by exercise, so a person can be fat and have no eating disorder—and no health problem either. What may be overfat for one person may be fine for someone else of the same height.

The number on the scale is only one measure, and not a very accurate one. The familiar insurance company "weight tables" are derived from averaging the weights of thousands of policyholders; they tell us what the averages are but not what is healthy. They were never intended to serve as absolute standards of healthy weight. A better measure is the *percentage* of body weight that is fat, which professional health care providers can calculate using calipers (small devices that pinch the flesh at certain points on the body) or underwater weighing.

Debate continues over how much excess weight constitutes a health risk. Diabetes and heart conditions are among the diseases worsened by extreme obesity. But some researchers feel that the moderately obese are in no worse danger than those of "normal" weight. And they may be in less danger than the extremely thin or those who purge, or whose weight has fluctuated dramatically for years. In any thousand people, some will be thin, many will be considered "average" size, and some will be fat. Unfortunately, cultural prejudices can generate fear of fat, an affliction that can strike "average-sized" or even thin people.

When people become obese through compulsive eating, they do have an eating disorder. Some of these compulsive eaters add weight as a shield or a weapon. Says one obese person:

Fat becomes your protection from anything you need protection from: men, women, sexuality (blossoming or developed), frightening feelings of any sort. It becomes your rebellion, your way of telling your parents, your lovers, the society around you, that you don't have to be who they want you to be. Fat becomes your way of talking. It says: I need help, go away, come closer, I can't, I won't, I'm angry, I'm sad. It becomes your vehicle for dealing with every problem you have.[4]

Yet fat can be hated, too, as shown by the following poem, written by a woman who has since made substantial progress with her problem:

You surround me. You smother me. You insult me.
Because of you, I am self-conscious—afraid to meet people;
Afraid of their opinion of me.
You turn me into a vast object—able to converse with either sex, because I have no sex.
I hate you. I hate myself for creating you.
You make me tired, exhausted.
I can't see my feet—can't tie my shoe laces—can't bend down.

I feel dowdy and useless, a gargantuan vegetable.
You are a parasite, a leech sapping my strength.
People think I am simple because of you.
They mouth their words and talk slowly and loudly at me.
I always end up doing the washing up at parties —
Glad to escape from the food and the trivial conversation
To the comparative haven of peace of the kitchen.

But now the tables are turning.
I'm slowly murdering you.
I can pinch you.
It is as if I could take my French cook's knife
And slice you to pieces.

You are gradually disappearing from my body and my
life.
How I abhor you.
You are my fat.[5]

A true eating disorder has less to do with fat, or the amount
and quality of food eaten, than with the thinking and emotions
underlying choices a person makes.

The Question of Labels

Eating disorders are not on-off conditions like pregnancy or
measles: a person can be a little bit eating disordered, or mildly
eating disordered, or severely eating disordered. For instance,
one person may eat three meals a day. Another might eat a big
breakfast, skip lunch, and have a light dinner. A third might
skip breakfast and snack the rest of the day. All of these eating
habits might be perfectly healthy and acceptable, depending on
what each person ate.

Other patterns are less desirable. A woman binges once a
year, or goes on a crash diet in anticipation of her class reunion,
or overeats just before her period, or bores her friends with
diet talk. Still, these are not eating disorders. More problematic
is the man who often feels out of control but never actually
binges or purges, or a dieter who may deprive herself of necessary nutrients. But none of these people has an eating disorder either.

Someone we *do* consider to have an eating disorder diets
relentlessly, to the point of emaciation, or can't stop eating, or
throws up regularly. Food controls her life.

Because of these variations, even experts—using in-depth
interviews, medical evaluations, and sophisticated psychological tests—must struggle to find whether a given person has an
actual, diagnosable eating disorder. The person being evaluated can forget, distort, be embarrassed, try to please the researcher, mean different things for the same words, or not

understand the question. Thus, the observer's ability to gauge the extent of another's problem cannot be perfect.

Even two patients with the same diagnosed eating disorders are not identical. One person labeled "bulimic" binges and purges three times a day, another once a week. One called "anorexic" is 30 percent underweight and denies there is a problem; another is 20 percent underweight and tries but fails to eat.

While knowledge in the eating disorders field is expanding rapidly, and we have learned to define and diagnose anorexia and bulimia with some confidence, such labels should be used with caution, especially by a layperson. A careful assessment by a professional is needed before a sure diagnosis can be made.

Are Eating Disorders Curable?

At seventeen, Alice was five feet, eight inches and weighed eighty-nine pounds. She had been a "normal" child until thirteen, according to her mother. Then she decided to become a model and began dieting. Soon she was exercising compulsively and losing weight. When her father tried to force her to eat, she became obstinate, shook her head, and ran from the room. She couldn't understand why everyone tried to interfere with her desire to be thin and successful. Finally, just to keep them quiet, she would eat in front of the family, but would make herself throw up afterward. No one knew about this practice until the day she had a car accident brought on by faintness. At the hospital she was diagnosed as having advanced malnutrition, but it was too late. She died ten days later.

Malvena was also seventeen when she came to the attention of health professionals. She came from a well-to-do family, in which the children always went to college and pursued prestigious careers. She did well in school, and her report cards always contained remarks such as "very agreeable and hard-working." During her senior year in high school she began staying up late to study for exams. The school counselor noticed she seemed tired and thin. But Malvena denied anything was wrong. One day, however, she fainted in class and was taken to the hospital, where she was given a physical examination and found to be significantly underweight. She had hidden her extreme thinness under loose clothing. In addition, her blood chemistry was unbalanced. With encouragement, she entered an outpatient eating disorder program and began to improve.

These two cases, with their different endings, hint at the variety of outcomes of eating disorders. Some people get well with professional help, some people improve without it, and some do not get well despite professional help. And a few die. These latter tragedies sometimes receive publicity out of proportion to their numbers, yet they do highlight the real dangers of anorexia.

The publicity over eating disorders in recent years has helped many sufferers to realize that problems with food are widespread and harmful. Unfortunately, some articles and broadcasts have sensationalized them, dwelling on extreme cases and painting a bleak picture of the sufferer's prospects.

Despite the serious nature of advanced eating disorders, it must be emphasized that *recovery is possible.* The recovery may be difficult. But we have seen people with serious and long-standing problems recover from bulimia, anorexia, and other eating problems. Our colleagues in hospitals, clinics, and universities in this country and abroad have made great strides in understanding and treating eating problems during the short time eating problems have been officially recognized as physical and psychological disorders. The Twelve Step group, Overeaters Anonymous, has become increasingly sophisticated (allowing for more individually tailored eating styles). This way, it reaches out to even more of the eating disordered to offer hope and support.

Recovery

Our definition of *recovery* includes these elements:

1. Eating behavior and relationship to food become more natural.
2. Thinking about food and body becomes less obsessive.
3. Physical health is restored.
4. Body image becomes more accurate.
5. Self-esteem and respect for the body increase.
6. More constructive problem-solving skills are learned as well as used.

Recovery does not mean "has a perfect figure forever," "never thinks about food again," or "now eats perfectly at all times." The recovered person will live in the real world, like everyone else, with an imperfect body and occasional unwelcome thoughts, some of which may be about food. She will probably never have the "perfect" model's figure—few people do. A recovered person is likely to look back with amazement that she could have used food so destructively and given slimness such exaggerated importance, when there are other things in life she has learned to value and enjoy.

CHAPTER 5

What Causes Eating Disorders?

Most of us use food to ease us through the highs and lows of life. We celebrate with food; we console ourselves with food. Everyone has uncomfortable feelings and difficult situations to cope with on occasion, and a food treat can be very consoling. For some people, however, the food seems to be in charge.

> *Geneva was the eldest of six children. Her father developed cancer of the pancreas when she was sixteen, so her first year in college was full of worry about him and about younger brothers and sisters at home. There was not enough money for frequent telephone calls or flights back to her hometown. In addition, her schoolwork was much harder than she had expected. Geneva began to overeat at the dormitory where she lived, and soon her life revolved around meals and snacks.*

What has caused Geneva to misuse food? For her, as for most people with eating disorders, there are several main sources. First, the cultural environment sets the stage: our national fatness phobia and obsession with appearances pressure people to restrict eating. Second, family style can contribute to the eating disorder. The family may be competitive, or concerned with appearances, or perfectionistic, or it may deny emotions. In this atmosphere, a person is more apt to misuse food. Third, the biological effects of severe or erratic dieting can turn tentative experiments with food abuse into full-fledged problems.

Cultural Factors

The primary culprit in creating disordered attitudes about food is our culture's dread of fat. A person with an eating disorder has probably accepted the popular idea that the perfect life can only be lived in the perfect body. Countless Americans judge themselves by television commercials, magazine ads, and movie images. Yet the carefully selected and made-up models they see artfully photographed represent only the thinnest 5 percent of our population. Moreover, a certain moralistic tone enters the picture with the recent emphasis on health. Exercise and calorie control are not only necessary for appearance's sake. They are now touted as being good for us—"you must be bad if you aren't doing what is good for you." To an anxious person, weight thus acquires yet another possible meaning, that of looking imprudent as well as unattractive.

Society (as represented by movies, advertising, peer pressure, family tradition) is eager to remind us that fat is somehow wrong—self-indulgent, unhealthy, vulgar. We often ridicule and punish others who are fat. And when we gain a few extra pounds we punish ourselves. In this atmosphere eating disorders flourish. If our society did not fear fat, we would not see nearly so many eating disorders. The millions of people who diet all their lives to avoid the dreaded fate of being fat attest to the depth of this prejudice. Susan C. Wooley and O. Wayne Wooley, authors of "Should Obesity Be Treated At All?" write:

> *Many [obesity] treatment successes are in fact condemned to a life of weight obsession, semistarvation, and all the symptoms produced by chronic hunger ... some consume as few as 800 calories per day, struggle constantly to ward off or compensate for losses of control, and seem precariously close to*

developing a frank eating disorder. Perceptible beneath the visible pride is often an unmistakable bitterness over the price they pay to have a socially acceptable body. If this is, indeed, a better fate than being fat, it only shows how miserable we have made the world for fat people.[1]

Like many people trying to avoid this dreaded fate, Geneva thinks she has discovered a clever loophole in the supposed "law" of eat and gain. If she vomits her excess food, she can have her "anesthetic," yet not suffer for it. As she would later tell us ruefully, she was "eating her cake and heaving it too."

Of course, there are risks. The digestive mechanism does not willingly go into reverse. It protests, and repercussions are created with disorders of the heart, intestines, blood chemistry, gall bladder, and teeth.

Another risk is that the habit is hard to give up. Although eating disorders start in the mind, they can soon have the body imprisoned in a self-perpetuating cycle. In the words of one authority, an eating disorder eventually takes on "a life of its own."[2] For example, a bulimic may find that the release of purging becomes an end in itself. Or an hour after bingeing on sugar, an overeater, for biological reasons, may feel a renewed craving for sugar. It requires a lot of work to escape from these vicious cycles.

The Biochemical Connection

Research has shown that chronic semistarvation can lead to an amazing array of effects on the body and mind. During World War II, researcher Ancel Keys and co-workers gained permission to arrange a research project using conscientious objectors. The men were observed and studied for three months while they ate normal amounts. Then for six months they were restricted to half their normal intake, and finally for three months they were gradually re-fed. Keys found that, while deprived, the men became obsessed with food. They hoarded their food, dragged meals out for hours, and began to use spices and chewing gum. They studied cookbooks, and three of them changed careers afterward to work with food. They became depressed and their self-esteem plummeted. Some of them found ways to pilfer food or to binge. These effects lasted for months, even after they were given free access to food and their weights normalized.[3]

Keys found the following effects of starvation:

Attitudes and behavior toward food
Food preoccupation
Collecting recipes, menus, books
Unusual eating habits
Increased use of coffee, tea, spices
Bingeing

Emotional and social effects
Depression, anxiety, irritability
Lability (unstable moods)
Psychotic episodes (periods of hallucination, gross distortions in thinking, or generally losing touch with what we call reality)
Personality changes
Social withdrawal

Cognitive changes
Lowered ability to concentrate
Apathy
Poor judgment

Physical changes
Sleep disturbances
Weakness
Gastrointestinal tract disturbances
Edema (retaining water)

Hypothermia (low body temperature)
Paresthesia (itching, burning, or tickling skin
    sensations)
Reduced sex drive
Decreased basal metabolism rate[4]

Later studies have confirmed that prolonged deprivation can create effects such as these in a person's mind, body, and relationships.

The Dieting Myth

Dieting, we now know, actually helps to create eating disorders! Tinkering with one's natural eating pattern almost always starts before the eating disorder and is the first step toward the creation of poor habits. A misguided effort to control fat produces changes in the body, which produce effects on thinking processes, which in turn fix the abuse of food in place as a habit.

Reducing calorie intake signals the body to slow down and use fuel more efficiently. Thus, after an initial weight loss (which, in fact, represents mostly water) the dieter finds herself stranded on a plateau, unable to lose more no matter how strictly she diets. And she gets hungry. To add insult to injury, research has shown that weight returns more quickly when normal eating is resumed after a period of starvation. When this process has been started and abandoned a few times, the dieter often finds herself heavier than ever, with weight harder to lose and easier to regain.[5]

Despite bitter experience, a person tends to try the same solution again, with only minor variations. If diet A didn't work, maybe diet B will. When diet B fails, try diet C. Or a more dangerous and radical solution may occur to the frustrated dieter: shutting off appetite altogether with drugs, such as amphetamines, cocaine, or nicotine. But these drugs, like dieting itself, disrupt bodily systems and the dieter may even become dangerously drug dependent.

Two regulatory mechanisms govern food use in the human body. The *metabolism* (ruled by the thyroid and the rest of the endocrine system) determines how efficiently we burn food. A more conserving metabolism is a blessing in times of uncertain food supply, because it makes maximum use of the fuel available and maintains a higher proportion of fat in the body. Body fat requires less fuel (calories) than muscle. A less conserving metabolism, by contrast, requires more fuel per pound of body weight, rather like an inefficient furnace, and overall more fuel is required each day to maintain that body. People with less conserving metabolisms would be at greater risk in time of famine. But in our culture of plenty and slimness mania, they are considered "lucky" because they can eat all they want without gaining weight.

The other regulatory mechanism is the *set point,* which governs fat ratio in a person's body. The set point, rather than having a central location, seems to consist of an interaction among brain centers, fat cells, and hormones. This "committee" decides how much fat it wants your body to have. Your conscious mind has no say in the matter. If your mind (influenced by advertisements of slim models) tries to overrule the set point, the set point will generally win.

It has several ways of doing this. One way is to "defend" the desired fat ratio by consuming lean body tissue (muscle, organs, even brain tissue) rather than burning fat to fuel daily activities. Another is to squeeze more calories out of the same amount of food, creating the dreaded diet plateau. The body seems to have a will of its own, which has ways of defeating the diet-obsessed mind.

There is some good news, though. The "escape clause" from this disheartening law is exercise. Regular aerobic exercise of a specified duration can readjust the set point, changing the way the body uses fuel and increasing its demand for calories.

Before these discoveries, there was no way to explain why diets failed. But now we know more about how the body works and how very difficult weight loss and the maintenance of the loss can be. Two researchers studying traditional dieting concluded wryly: "Perhaps dieting is the disorder we should be attempting to cure."[6]

When weight must be lost for health or other reasons, we can now use our knowledge to help the patient preserve muscle mass and good nutrition. We encourage her to exercise aerobically to help readjust her set point, and learn a satisfying, healthy, low-fat way to eat for the rest of her life.

Premenstrual Tensions

Perhaps here is the place to mention that some women experience genuine premenstrual tensions that seem to intensify their food cravings, depression, or loss of control. These little-understood biochemical fluctuations are beginning to attract serious medical attention, and treatments are now being developed and are available in some places.

Family Sources

Family patterns may contribute to eating disorders. Generally, the families of anorexics tend to be too close, too dedicated to perfection and keeping up appearances, and too polite to address conflict directly. Families of bulimics tend to experience more conflict and tragedy, with more divorces, alcoholism, obesity, and depression. Such broad generalizations do not apply to the family of every patient. But they help investigators and therapists hypothesize about what stresses and faulty beliefs an eating disordered patient may be living with, and determine what steps to take to help the family.

Personality and Personal History

People with certain personalities seem particularly vulnerable to eating disorders. Perhaps much of this is pure temperament: some babies are born placid and content, while others struggle with life from the outset. Some patients can point to specific traumas that set off abnormal eating, such as the death of a parent or being molested. Others remember being hurt by the accumulation of everyday slights. Whatever the sources, characteristics like suppressing emotion, perfectionism, and desire to please do play a part.

Most people with eating disorders are conscientious, hard-working, and nice. They are forever comparing, caretaking, putting themselves down, putting their own needs last, and doing without nurturing from themselves and others. They seem to have set themselves apart: happiness doesn't seem attainable for them. Food is not only a consolation but a further danger.

A few eating disordered patients come from doting families, and can't understand why the world is less indulgent of them than their families were. They are wracked by insecurity in relationships. And they have difficulty making decisions, because they grew up expecting to succeed at everything.

A difficult current situation, or even an event long past, can contribute to an eating disorder. Many patients report past histories of sexual victimization—molestation in childhood, or rape or battering in adult life. These shocking traumas can cause people to retreat into private worlds of unhealthy eating. But more normal losses and separations from significant people can also lead to disordered eating. Even welcome life changes—leaving home for college, getting married, or starting a new job—can cause stress. As famed researcher Hans Selye found, too much stress can impact health in many ways. Research on stresses among eating disordered patients shows many patients recently lost a relationship, faced a sexual conflict, or moved within six months of the onset of their disorder.[7]

Paul, a distinguished-looking gentleman in his fifties, is portly and becoming more so. Not only is his blood pressure high, he also has a family history of diabetes. How can he tell his wife about his night eating, or how he sometimes eats all day at his office? His doctor has recommended weight loss several times, but this strategy just doesn't work, for Paul eats compulsively, and trying to restrain himself backfires into bigger binges. He worries about his health, but doesn't know what to do. He can't bring himself to talk to his doctor about his eating habit.

Unlike some people with eating problems, Paul had been a skinny kid until his parents split up when he was twelve. Then, he and his mother and sister developed a way of being close together: they would get big bags of cookies and pretzels, and sit in front of the television watching favorite shows and commenting on them. Paul's mother, overwhelmed by responsibility and exhausted from long days at work, would buy hamburgers and fries for all, with ice cream thrown in on weekends. Eating became a ritualized way of keeping their anxiety at bay. They all put on weight, but since they were together, it didn't matter. They joked about it a bit, and when the outside world seemed indifferent, they relied on each other even more.

Certain lifestyles like Paul's encourage the formation of eating disorders. For instance, going to college may mean entering a competitive atmosphere for the first time, losing the childhood home, studying endlessly, and expecting great things socially. This can put enormous strain on anyone, especially a person with self-doubts. Add the dilemmas of making choices about sex, drugs, and roommates, and it is little wonder that college students are among those hardest hit by eating disorders.

Another common hothouse for eating disorders is traditional marriage, as experienced by the wife who is a full-time homemaker. She is faced with a nearby refrigerator, small children who must be fed many times a day, repetitive, low-prestige tasks, and isolation from the pleasure of adult contact and working with others. Food can become her job and her friend.

Habit

Overeating or throwing up get "rehearsed" many times a day. One reason recovery from an eating disorder can take so long is that a daily habit is being challenged. A compulsive eater who has binged three times a day for five years has practiced the behavior more than five thousand times. Eating or purging has become a way of coping—a positive reinforcer and a way to escape painful feelings or thoughts. Gradually, new, positive reinforcers must be tried and added to the person's repertoire. Twelve Step programs like Overeaters Anonymous can be enlisted to help instill a new habit of joining others for support, sharing, and strength for overcoming the destructive habit.

> *Kate was the second oldest of five children. Her older sister was sickly, and Kate soon became a "little mother" with the younger children. Her father worked two jobs and was away a lot, and even when he was at home he seemed to be off in a world of his own, with little time or energy for his wife. Kate sensed this and tried to fill the gap.*
>
> *She needed to be with people, and felt hungry and empty when she was alone. At age twelve, she began to use food to fill her own emptiness, but this made her feel fat and embarrassed to be around people. Two years later, she discovered she could throw up and keep her weight down.*
>
> *Kate always got good grades at school. Her mother had ambitions for her, and always insisted that Kate could do anything she wanted to. Her Uncle Ralph, a wealthy self-made businessman, was held up to her as an example of what a person can do if he tries hard enough. Once when Kate was upset over placing second in a skating competition, her parents*

contended that she would be giving in to weakness by com-plaining or feeling low. Someone like Uncle Ralph would just dig in and improve for next time—no room for self-pity! So Kate swallowed her disappointment and vowed not to let her parents down again by being weak.

For Kate, the causes of her eating disorder were primarily of the "family history" sort, though let's not forget the personality factor. She believed she had to be acceptable to everyone, to follow all the rules, to take care of others—traits that encourage people to turn to food for solace.

Since eating disorders have so many causes, no one factor can be "blamed" for creating an eating disorder in a particular person. Accordingly, treatment usually addresses many aspects of the patient's life.

CHAPTER 6

Eating Disorders Can Make You Sick

Eating disorders can create very real medical problems, from mild to life-threatening. Some medical complications, such as tooth deterioration and menstrual irregularities, do not qualify as emergencies, though they should be treated. Other situations to be discussed later in this chapter require prompt medical attention.

Milder Discomforts

The eating disordered person tends to be most aware of the day-to-day symptoms she experiences. An anorexic, for example, may need to urinate frequently. She may become preoccupied with trips to the bathroom, which can be especially inconvenient at nighttime. She also tends to feel cold, since she doesn't have enough fat to insulate her body. You may see her wearing several sweaters and a coat on even a mild day. She may find sitting uncomfortable, since her tailbone comes into painful contact with the chair. She may seek soft sofas and chairs, or carry a pillow or rolled-up sweatshirt wherever she goes.

Anorexics and bulimics sometimes feel dizzy or "spacey." Chronic undereating, or vomiting food after eating, leaves the brain famished and unable to do its job properly. The famished person feels light-headed and tired, and needs extra effort to perform tasks. Some anorexics and bulimics drink huge amounts of water, tea, coffee, or diet drinks, which further contributes to a spaced-out feeling and abnormal body chemistry. A small meal delivers glucose to the brain within half an hour, and this can relieve some symptoms. But it is a temporary solution. Contrary to what some bulimics or anorexics believe, one meal or one good day of eating is not enough! Malnutrition and blood chemistry imbalances must be corrected with months of adequate nutrition.

The Body's Response to Dangerous Eating Practices

What is going on in the body when a person starves, binges, or purges? Researchers are finding very complex interactions of the body's digestive, circulatory, reproductive, and nervous systems. *Starving* deprives the body of needed nutrients. The body must then draw on stored energy. Glycogen from the liver supplies some energy, but this is soon depleted. You would think the stored fat would come to the rescue and supply energy—after all, isn't that what fat is for? Unfortunately, the body consumes lean tissue (muscles, organs, even the heart) along with fat, within a few days of calorie deprivation. This explains why a person on a severe diet can feel tired and weak. Starving also affects many body functions: The heart rate slows and the blood pressure goes down. The thyroid also slows, which in turn slows the metabolism. Hair and skin growth decline, as do cell regeneration and replacement.

Bingeing, meanwhile, strains the body's resources, and may cause sleepiness and stomach dilation. In extreme cases stomach rupture—a very dangerous condition—can occur.

Purging is harmful if frequent or prolonged. Habitual vomiting can lead to tooth erosion, irritated or torn lining of stomach or esophagus, gall bladder problems, kidney damage from dehydration. Other complaints include back pain, menstrual irregularities, altered balances in blood chemicals, and a sense of fatigue and depletion.

Some overeaters try to undo the effects of their eating by using *laxatives* (which are intended to relieve constipation). Laxative abuse can lead to dependence on laxatives, constipation, bloating, and irritation or disease of the small intestine and colon. Dehydration and imbalance in the blood chemistry can also result from laxative abuse.

If a person alternates or combines these behaviors—such as following a period of bingeing with a period of starvation—the body may develop a combination of painful and unhealthy conditions.

Medical Emergencies

Since starving, bingeing, and purging upset the body's normal functioning, medical emergencies can occasionally arise.

> *Tabitha, seventeen, complained of abdominal pain. She began to look pale, her pulse rate accelerated, and her breathing was shallow. Medical examination revealed that she had a hiatal hernia (upward displacement of the stomach into the chest). In addition, she had swallowed a rubber band she wrapped around her finger to help induce vomiting.*

> *Karen was found leaning against a wall in the stairwell of her high school, trying to catch her breath. She was trying to get to her next class, and had become too tired to climb the stairs. She had been vomiting so much that her blood chemistry was disturbed, leading her to feel dizzy.*

> *Amy had felt chest pains for about a week. One night they became very sharp just as she was getting ready for bed. Frightened, she told her husband. After asking a neighbor to watch their children, Amy and her husband went to the local hospital's emergency room. Luckily, it was not a heart attack but an unpleasant side-effect of malnutrition.*

The more serious medical conditions must be treated at once. Be alert for complaints of headache, dizziness, shortness of breath, weakness, blood in the stool, and acute abdominal distress. They may indicate one or more of the following conditions:

1. *Dehydration.* A common result of chronic vomiting, dehydration causes headaches, dizziness on rising, and even fainting. The abuse of laxatives, diuretics (drugs that encourage urination), and fasting can make this problem worse. If the dehydration is severe, hospitalization may be warranted. A person with milder complaints of dizziness or headaches should see a doctor. If the person is fainting, she should be brought to the emergency room.
2. *Blood chemistry (electrolyte) imbalance.* The balance of basic elements needed for proper functioning of the nervous system can be upset by repeated vomiting. The potassium level is particularly critical. If it is low, the person can feel weak or dizzy. In extreme cases, cardiac arrest can occur. Electrolyte problems are always suspected in cases of weakness or dizziness, and medical supervision is essential.
3. *Ipecac-related complications.* Ipecac is an over-the-counter drug used to induce vomiting in poisoning emergencies. A few bulimics misuse it to stimulate vomiting. If any Ipecac remains in the system after purging, it can damage the heart muscle. Since most purging is incomplete, repeated Ipecac use can lead to serious problems, even death. An Ipecac abuser is likely to need inpatient treatment.
4. *Laxative abuse.* The lower gastrointestinal tract (colon) is meant to eliminate the indigestible parts of food, and it normally functions without special attention. But some people with eating disorders overuse laxatives to get rid of excess calories (or even calories their bodies need). The actual caloric value of food ejected in this way is minimal, since most nutrients are absorbed earlier in the digestive process, in the small intestine. Furthermore, daily use of laxatives upsets the normal functioning of the digestive tract, and increasingly large doses are required to produce an effect. This can

lead to dependence. Potassium levels can be drastically reduced by laxative overdoses, causing weakness and dizziness. Worse, laxatives can cause intestinal cramping or even
internal bleeding. All these problems require medical
attention.

5. *Foreign objects.* A rare emergency involves accidental swallowing of such objects as toothbrushes some bulimics use to
assist vomiting. These can damage or rupture the esophagus. Prompt medical attention is required.

6. *Acute abdominal pain.* In a person with advanced anorexia or
bulimia, abdominal pain should be taken very seriously. After ruling out menstrual cramps, indigestion, and other normal causes, the doctor will check for stomach or esophageal
rupture, an inflamed pancreas, gall bladder attacks, or hiatal
hernia.

7. *Low weight.* Extreme emaciation, the cardinal sign of anorexia, occurs with some bulimics also. Low weight may
prevent onset of menstruation and create poor conditions
for bone maintenance. Prolonged starvation can lead to death.
A person of very low weight should be monitored regularly
by a physician, preferably one who understands eating disorders. If your anorexic friend's health is in danger—if she
is too weak to walk upstairs or out of the house—bring her
to an emergency room or doctor at once, by ambulance if
necessary. Sometimes those who are concerned about an
eating disordered person must intervene to stop the starvation over her protests that she is quite all right. She may be
too weak to walk up stairs or open heavy doors and still
insist she is fine.

It is unlikely that one person would suffer from all of the
medical consequences on this sobering list. But it does show
the great range of possible risks a person with an eating disorder may be running. Recognizing health danger signs is particularly important if the eating disordered person is a child or
adolescent, since the adult is responsible for securing medical
attention.

Keep a list of locations and phone numbers of nearby emergency rooms and hospitals with special units for treating eating disorders. By taking such precautions, you can be prepared for true emergencies and will be less likely to interfere or panic unnecessarily.

For these and for other, more chronic conditions, such as chronic fatigue, dizziness, or menstrual irregularities, ongoing medical care should be secured.

CHAPTER 7

Helping the Eating Disordered Person Begin Treatment

Now that you know something about eating disorders, let us walk you through the process of helping your friend or relative recover. The first question to ask is, does she, in fact, have an eating disorder?

When You Suspect She Is Bingeing, Purging, or Restricting

Many food-obsessed people keep their problem a secret, even from family or close friends. How can you know if a problem exists?

What to Look For
- Does she eat quite a bit more food than you would suspect for someone of her weight and activity level? This may be perfectly normal for her or it may be a sign of purging.
- Have her eating habits changed dramatically?
- Does she seem to eat little or nothing at mealtimes?
- Does she now eat radically different foods than she used to, that is, only diet foods, or only vegetables and fruits?
- Have you discovered her eating in secret?
- Does food disappear from the kitchen more rapidly than you would expect, especially sweets and white flour carbohydrates such as white bread and white pasta?
- Is she spending excessive time in the bathroom?

- Are there laxatives or emetics (vomit-inducing drugs) in the bathroom?
- Does she avoid social occasions where food is served?
- Does she talk excessively about food and figures?
- Does she have more dental problems than usual (one sign of chronic vomiting)?
- Does she make a lot of self-deprecating remarks, especially about her body, calling it fat, ugly, bad?
- Has she gained or lost a lot of weight recently or repeatedly?

No single factor determines that she has an eating disorder. But if several occur together, it is reasonable to investigate further. If the answers to these questions confirm your sense that something is wrong, two delicate tasks await you: (1) bringing up the subject with your child or spouse or friend, and (2) persuading her to get treatment.

> *When Karen began to diet at age fourteen, her mother, Ann, watched with amusement. It was a phase all girls go through, Ann thought. When at fifteen Karen was still dieting regularly and complaining when she regained weight, Ann wasn't really very worried. But then, around Karen's sixteenth birthday Ann began to see ominous signals. Karen seemed to stay in the bathroom a long time after meals, and looked pale and drawn. Ann also noticed that Karen complained about her weight and figure constantly. The dentist mentioned to Ann that Karen's teeth were worse than they had been in years. Ann became suspicious. When she confronted her daughter about the eating problems, Karen fortunately answered honestly and Ann's worst fears were confirmed. She brought Karen in for treatment the next week.*

Not all people with eating disorders can talk about their problem as easily as Karen. Some hide the seriousness of the problem from themselves and their loved ones for a long time. But there are visible signs to look for.

An anorexic is very thin, surprisingly active, and perfectionistic. He or she denies that anything is wrong and is puzzled by everyone's concern. The anorexic often feels cold even when the room is adequately heated.

A bulimic—who is frequently of normal weight—may look perfectly well. But sometimes in a serious stage of the illness, the bulimic can look pale, tired, distracted, and unhealthy. Like the anorexic, the bulimic tends to give a good school or job performance, but she is self-critical anyway. She tends to worry about people's opinions and to take care of others' needs. You might notice the poor condition of her teeth or occasional dizziness. Food disappearing from the refrigerator is a sign, as are frequent or lengthy bathroom trips.

A compulsive eater can't seem to stay away from food, whether it be in large quantities or small. She is constantly "grazing." She may be heavy, or she may be using some means such as intense exercising or purging to remain at a lower weight. She may ask you to help restrain her by doing such things as locking the refrigerator or cautioning her against overindulging.

Again, these indicators only *suggest* that an eating disorder exists. A professional evaluation is needed to confirm or rule out the diagnosis.

It's No Secret

One day Paul, the portly man we met in Chapter Five, found himself talking to a consultant at one of the commercial weight-loss programs—the fifth one he'd tried—about his food problems. She listened sympathetically. She was wise enough to understand that he had more problems than the diet program could solve, and suggested he see a counselor she could recommend. He decided to go.

Paul was nervous at first about being "in therapy." He couldn't really explain it to his wife. He told her that work had become very demanding and he needed counseling for "stress." After a few months, he still couldn't work up the nerve to explain it to her. Then he had an "accident" that helped him to reveal the emotional problems underlying his eating disorder. He asked her to help with filling out insurance forms, and the reason for his therapy was there on the papers. Secretly, he was relieved to have it out in the open. Now that he was making progress, he could tell her about his therapy as something that was already working.

Her response surprised him. She said she'd suspected something was wrong and just didn't know what. She thought maybe the marriage had run dry and he didn't love her as before. She was relieved to hear it wasn't about her! She supported him in going to therapy as long as he needed, and even went with him to two sessions.

Little did Paul know his wife would be so receptive. You, too, may be able to speed your loved one's journey toward recovery by supporting the idea of inner exploration in therapy.

The best way to begin helping an eating disordered person is to choose a time when you are unlikely to be interrupted, and lay your cards on the table. Tell her that you know something is wrong, and ask if she wants to talk about it.

This can be scary. Let us walk you through it.

1. *State your concern.* "I'm worried about you."
2. *Invite her to open up.* "Is there something bothering you?"
3. *Assure her you respect her limits.* "You don't have to tell me everything, but I care about you and I want to help."
4. *Present the evidence, trying not to sound accusatory. Just bring up the facts.* "You never eat with us anymore." "You spend so much time in the bathroom." "There are so many laxatives in the cabinet now."
5. *Leave time to listen.*
6. *Assure her that she can get help.* "People get over eating disorders. You don't have to live with this forever, but you'll need to get some help for it."

This is a lot of territory to cover, and she may not let you get all the way through it at once. Give her time to absorb all parts of your message. Body language is important, so sit in a relaxed but attentive manner, making nonthreatening but direct eye contact. Then be prepared to listen as nonjudgmentally as you can, helping her feel safe to speak if she wishes.

If she denies having a problem, there is nothing you can do to get her to acknowledge it. But you can work to keep open the channels of communication. Perhaps you can say something like, "You may not want to talk about this now, but I'm here if you need me. Remember what I'm saying and let's keep talking."

If she is your minor child, a visit to a pediatrician, family physician, or a therapist specializing in eating disorders may be desirable. That way, you can express your concerns and help her get professional assistance.

If you feel therapy would help an adult friend or relative, suggest it. You can point out that many people have eating disorders, and good results are being achieved in treatment. Your friend may be feeling hopeless, isolated, or weird about herself because of her problem. Such assurances can be heartening.

Finding Professional Help

1. *The initial phone call.* Ideally, the person with an eating disorder should make the first step to find help. But you can pave the way by surveying eating disorder therapists in your area, and learning their fees and schedules. Your physician, local or state psychological association, hospital with an eating disorder program, or Yellow Pages can provide a start. National organizations can also help.
2. *Choosing a therapist.* You may have heard of different "brands" of psychotherapy: psychoanalytic, psychodynamic, cognitive-behaviorist, humanistic, Gestalt, family therapy, and more. These are different approaches to dealing with human

problems. Each has its own theories and techniques. A therapist's choice of technique represents his or her best judgment about how people get into difficulties and how to get them out. Many therapists combine two or more approaches.

Each state has licensing laws that govern the practice of therapy. In California, for instance, trained therapists have one of four licenses: (1) A psychiatrist is a medical doctor (M.D.), can prescribe medication and may also provide psychotherapy. (2) A psychologist has a doctorate (Ph.D.) in psychology. (3) Marriage, family, and child counselors have master's degrees (M.A.) in a human services field. (4) Social workers have a master's degree (M.S.W.) in social work. All have extensive field training, have passed rigorous state examinations, and are qualified to provide psychotherapy. They are called Board Certified Psychiatrists; Licensed Clinical Psychologists; Marriage, Family, and Child Counselors (M.F.C.C.); or Licensed Clinical Social Workers (L.C.S.W.). Be sure that any professional you consult is board-certified or licensed.

Psychiatrists tend to have the highest range of fees, psychologists the second highest, and master's level professionals the lowest. Insurance policies in many cases reimburse part of the cost of counseling. Many therapists have sliding scales, charging their clients according to income. If you're choosing among equally qualified professionals, it is advisable to select the one who gives the patient a sense of rapport and mutual understanding.

3. *Your Role.* If the adult patient is extremely shy or nervous, you may have the urge to call to make the first appointment, or even to accompany her to the therapist's office. In our experience, this may help in rare cases. But it does not guarantee that her venture into therapy will "take" at this time. The more active role you take in steering a person into therapy, the more it begins to seem like it is your project rather than hers.

The younger the person, the greater your responsibility. A

twelve-year-old daughter needs your help in making the appointment and keeping it. But older adolescents and adults respond better if they initiate contact. A twenty-eight-year-old spouse often does best with a gentle suggestion rather than a pushing or parental approach. But if the light, permissive touch isn't working and the illness is life-threatening, common sense is called for. Sometimes, you must put a child or adolescent into treatment over her objections, even if overprotectiveness may have been one of the original sources of the problem. You can't solve everything at once!

Therapy is a learning process. The person you are concerned about will discover things about herself and life, if all goes well. There will be some painful moments, but you need not feel you are driving your child or spouse into an ordeal to "fix" what's wrong with her. Rather, you will be helping to free her from a serious problem.

4. *Sharing your experiences.* You may also want to share helpful experiences you have had in therapy. Remember, her experience may be different from yours. And she may have worries or problems she has not shared with you or others.

5. *When to stop.* There is a fine line between being helpful and being overprotective. We have spoken to friends and families who were afraid that their attempts to help their loved ones begin therapy might just be part of the same old problem—"She'll come once, to please me." This might be true. But in the case of a minor child, or an adult whose illness has become life-threatening or who is referred by the courts because of offenses related to the eating disorder, it may be necessary to help her get treatment even if she resents it. You can try to help her get started in therapy. Then let the therapist continue the process.

We have found that a patient brought in by a parent or friend may be reluctant and not really want therapy. She may disappear after a few sessions. To prevent the frustration and failure such a turn of events can create, we say to her, "Let's agree to four sessions and then see how we're doing." This gives her a sense of participating in the decision, and lets her know she hasn't been sentenced indefinitely to something that was not her idea.

Jennifer had been at an East Coast college for just a month when her bulimia went from bad to worse. A straight-A student in high school, she was reacting to the pressures of college-level expectations by bingeing and purging. She called her mother long distance and poured out her feelings. Her mother, Jean, was naturally worried and felt bad about being far away. But communication between mother and daughter had always been good, so Jean asked if it would help if she scouted around for help.

Jennifer agreed, so Jean contacted the college counseling center and found that Jennifer was entitled to free group and individual therapy. Jean was also given a list of therapists in the community who specialized in treating people with eating disorders. Jean told her daughter the family would pay for private therapy if that was what Jennifer wanted. Jennifer chose to attend a therapy group at the counseling center and to also begin individual therapy with a psychologist there.

Three months later, her allotment of free individual sessions was used up. Jennifer then called two of the therapists in private practice that the center counselors had recommended. She met with each of them and decided to continue her individual therapy with the one she felt offered better rapport. Her bulimia was brought under control and by the end of her sophomore year was virtually gone.

Communicating with a Therapist

Therapists have a legal and ethical obligation to maintain their patients' privacy, and the therapeutic process depends heavily on this confidentiality. In some instances, however, you may be asked to take part in the process. For example, you may be invited to one or more sessions dealing with matters that concern you, or to help the therapist get a more complete picture of the eating disordered person's situation.

Minors

While a parent has a legal right to know that his or her minor child is in therapy and even to have access to some information, most parents agree to the need for privacy in the communication between therapist and patient. Make yourself available to the therapist in case of need. But don't expect to be given details of the therapeutic process. With child and adolescent patients, therapy often includes parents, especially as the therapist begins gathering information to evaluate the problem.

The patient will be advised of any contacts a parent makes with the therapist. This way, the therapist sets the example of open communication and protects the security of his or her relationship with the patient.

The Therapist's Obligations

The therapist has a duty to stop patients from harming themselves or others. This obligation includes reporting to appropriate agencies any threats a patient makes to harm herself or others, and hospitalizing the patient, if necessary. Never hesitate to report a suicide threat to the therapist working with your friend or relative. Instances of physical abuse or child neglect should also be reported.

Self-Help: An Alternative to Professional Therapy

Today in America, a person with a problem has many options. One of our most admirable national characteristics is our way of reaching out to one another in self-help groups. Cancer patients, war veterans, crime victims, job seekers, computer users—all these and more come together for mutual help. Whether it be a disease, a family problem, or social injustice, groups composed of people like yourself—your peers—can offer information, referrals, support, and a sense of belonging. In some cases, the group can take specific actions to help the individual, especially if established business, government, or medical systems have failed to provide assistance.

The eating disorder field also has its self-help services. For example, the American Anorexia/Bulimia Association (founded in 1978) offers two types of groups: one for eating disordered persons, led by a trained professional and a recovered anorexic or bulimic; and one for family members, led by a trained professional and the spouse, parent, or sibling of a recovered person.[1] The groups, which meet monthly, are intended as an adjunct to medical and psychological treatment. Peers can eventually lead these groups. This offers a kind of rite of passage for the person who has worked so hard to overcome the disorder, or is trying to understand a loved one who did. And seeing a recovered person now helping others encourages new members.

Self-help groups offer certain advantages. Among them are low cost (or no fee at all), a sense of equality, and responsiveness to members' needs. Shortcomings or failures in self-help groups may include tending to reinforce the "sick role" identity: "I am a bulimic (anorexic, compulsive eater) before I am anything else." This can delay a person trying to build a well-rounded, healthy personality. Inexperienced leaders can allow errors to occur: allowing nonproductive chatter, isolating a member who seems different, avoiding deep issues, blaming, and so on.

Twelve Step Groups

Alcoholics Anonymous is perhaps the most well-known self-help organization. The book *Alcoholics Anonymous*, also called the Big Book, describes the Twelve Steps on which an alcoholic's recovery program is based. These include acknowledging one's powerlessness over alcohol, taking an inventory of one's life and its effects on others, reconciling past mistakes, and appealing to a Higher Power. This source can be God, nature, or the wisdom within oneself. Programs based on the same principles have evolved to help people recover from addiction to other drugs, overeating, gambling, and other addictive behaviors.

Twelve Step programs help people "work the Steps" as they progress in their program "one day at a time." Essential to the process is peer support gained from attending meetings. The more meetings one can attend a week, the better. This gives a person nonjudgmental support of others who face the same problem. In beginning recovery, a common recommendation is "ninety meetings, ninety days." A participant can get additional support from a sponsor—a person further along in the program who can be relied on for guidance. The great support and caring available in the Twelve Step programs make them major sources of healing and recovery for people with addiction problems and for people who are close to someone with an addiction problem.

In the Overeaters Anonymous Twelve Step program, the person admits to being powerless over food. She surrenders to the care of a Higher Power to regain a sense of self and serenity. Turning one's problems over to a Higher Power can help break a vicious circle of self-blame and self-absorption. The sense of relief and reconnection to one's spiritual side can be profound.

O.A. considers food obsession, like alcoholism, to be incurable. But a person can hope to learn to adhere to a structured regime of regular meals.

In many cities, O.A. offers free group meetings which anyone may attend. A nonthreatening environment for sharing and healing is created. The group offers hope, support, and education for living a healthy lifestyle one day at a time. This way, the program can comfort people whose lives have become chaotic.

O.A. produces results for many people, but it may not be enough for everyone. Some need a more gradual change from unhealthy to healthier eating.

Paul went one step beyond his own therapy, and began giving talks at local schools about conquering food problems.

He assured the parents and children he spoke to that it wasn't
just a girl's issue and that boys had feelings and needs too. He
told them how no one had known his story until he was fifty-
four, and that was too long to keep a secret. He hoped that some
child out there would be spared the pain he had lived with
during the years he had used food as a drug.

Thus far we have tried to equip you to deal sensibly and
kindly with someone you may perceive as an eating disorder
victim. But you may feel that you are the victim and are wondering what help we can offer! We know you have needs too
(see Chapter 10). You have the right to run a normal household,
with regular work schedules, mealtimes, bedtimes, and appropriate responsibilities for each family member. The family should
conduct itself as part of the real world, even as family members
offer support for the eating disordered person's recovery.

Kate's entry into therapy was a story in itself. Her mother
came to town to visit, and with misgivings Joy confided her
worries. Kate's mother was surprised to hear about the problem, since Kate always sounded fine over the telephone.

Advising Kate of what they were doing, Joy and Kate's
mother called a local hospital for information about eating
disorders. What they heard made them think Kate would have
to check in for a prolonged stay, and this terrified Kate so much
that she refused to talk further about it. She thought it meant
she was a "mental case." But, afterward, she began to socialize
more and look better. Perhaps a good scare was all she needed!

But after a few weeks, she slumped again into depression
and bingeing. Joy lost patience with Kate when she came home
to a totally empty fridge again, and they had a fight. When Joy
stamped out of the apartment, Kate was distraught and horri-
fied at the thought of possibly losing her friend. She opened
the telephone book and called a local hospital. The person who
answered the phone talked to Kate for a while, and suggested
she call Dr. Harrison. She assured Kate that with Kate's permission she would also give Dr. Harrison Kate's phone number.

If Dr. Harrison was not in when Kate called, Dr. Harrison would call her. Kate didn't want to leave her phone number, so the person on the line said that was all right.

Fortunately, Dr. Harrison was in and could talk to Kate right away. She listened sympathetically, and her confident manner gave Kate a real feeling of hope. Perhaps here was someone who could help! They made an appointment for the following day.

Kate hadn't realized how much her life had deteriorated until she sat down to talk frankly with someone about it. And strangely enough, it was a relief. She told Dr. Harrison about her bingeing and purging, the way she took her roommate's food, the desperate attempts to stop. Dr. Harrison said Kate could call her Andrea, which made Kate feel more at ease.

During the first few sessions Kate did most of the talking, and things really began to make sense. As she told her life story and answered some of Andrea's questions, she realized that she had become an "assistant parent" at an early age and never felt she deserved to be taken care of, but rather took care of others.

Andrea also recommended a medical evaluation with Marla Goodstein, a medical doctor who also had a Ph.D. in nutrition. Kate reluctantly made the appointment, fearing the worst. Her blood was tested, and it turned out she was deficient in potassium and iron, and her body was low in muscle and high in fat, due in part to repeated crash dieting. Fortunately, her teeth had not decayed much, and Dr. Goodstein was able to reassure her that the puffiness around her cheeks and jaws would recede as she gave up purging. Her menstrual periods had become irregular, but there was no cause for great alarm, as restoring healthful eating—on a plan Kate and Dr. Goodstein worked out—could be expected to correct this.

Kate was glad Dr. Goodstein was so understanding about her fears. Kate had really been worried about her health for months. Until now, the more she worried, the more she binged and delayed doing anything about it. Andrea congratulated her on going to the doctor, and helped her understand the findings.

CHAPTER 8

How Professional Treatment Helps

When professional help is necessary, finding one's way through the maze of treatments can be a challenge. In this chapter we will describe many treatments and give you some sense of how to know when they are helping, and what to do if you have doubts.

Kinds of Treatment

There are many kinds of treatment for eating disorders: psychological, medical, and nutritional. The Twelve Step self-help programs provide a nonprofessional option (see previous chapter). These kinds of treatment are often used in combination.

Psychological. The psychological treatments you and your loved one will most likely encounter are individual therapy, group therapy, and family therapy. They are based on the idea that eating disorders originate from how we feel, think, and behave. They come from how we see the world, ourselves and others, and what we have learned to do to respond to life's difficulties. (We'll look more closely at them in a moment.)

Medical. Medical treatments include evaluation, nutritional rehabilitation, and medications (such as antidepressants). In extreme cases of starvation, tube feeding (delivering nourishing liquids directly to the stomach) and hyperalimentation (injecting nutrient-rich solutions into the bloodstream) have been used. Outpatient programs and inpatient hospital stays combine these medical treatments with group and individual psychotherapy.

Therapists who are medically trained (psychiatrists) may prescribe medication to relieve mental or physical discomforts associated with eating disorders, or to see a deeply depressed person through a crisis. If a patient is your minor child, make sure that the medication she is using is properly prescribed. Also be certain that the physician, if not her primary therapist, has contact with the primary therapist.

Antidepressants may be prescribed along with psychotherapy for the treatment of bulimia, on the theory that depression is a predisposing factor in the illness. Other medications can be used to reduce discomfort during recovery from anorexia and bulimia (for example, medications to relieve gastrointestinal symptoms).

A hospital stay can interrupt a person's entrenched daily cycle of bingeing, purging, or starving. It can also provide intensive learning and give her contact with fellow patients. See Chapter Nine for a fuller description of the hospital stay.

Nutritional Counseling. Incorrect ideas about eating abound in this culture. Bizarre weight-loss diets have become commonplace. Some people may actually believe consuming four hundred calories a day is sufficient; others may be frightened of certain foods that (they believe) instantly become dimply blobs of cellulite; others, in spite of knowing the calorie content of various foods, are not familiar with the nuances of nutritional balance and the body's needs. Millions of Americans have succumbed to the delusion that crash fasting will bring about permanent weight loss.

A nutritionist evaluates what patients have been eating, plans meals, and teaches them about their bodies' needs. Some hospital eating disorder treatment units even have kitchens in which patients plan, cook, and eat meals together.

Psychotherapy: How It Can Help

Let's take a closer look at how therapy can help your friend or relative think about eating in a more healthy manner.

Individual Therapy. Much of the therapy we have been describing in this book refers to ongoing, one-to-one arrangements between patient and therapist. This is the most common format for someone with a significant eating problem. The therapist may do many things: provide a sounding board; explore the patient's fears, conflicts, and beliefs about self and others; teach new coping skills; help her to decrease destructive behaviors; encourage her to question her negative self-image; and help her gain new skills to deal with the struggles of life.

> *Sylvia came to therapy distraught and unable to stop bingeing and purging. She admitted taking laxatives "once in a while" and using drugs "to help me sleep and relax." She was also worried by suicidal thoughts. She began individual therapy twice a week, and a family therapist saw her entire family once a week. Two months later, she was able to hand her laxatives and sleeping pills to her doctor and to join A.A. She realized she had been a pill abuser since early childhood.*
>
> *After six months, her suicidal thoughts decreased. She began to see how little she thought of herself, always trying to be the best and trying to never be seen as weak. Asking for help was "weak," not knowing the answer was "weak." Slowly, she began to let herself experiment with behaviors she had never tried. She let down her guard with her therapist and let herself cry over sad events in her past. She learned new ways to deal with feelings so that she didn't have to use drugs or food. She began to binge less and even when she binged, it felt less important, less horrid.*

Long-term Psychotherapy. The long-term psychotherapy patient will probably meet with a therapist one or more times a week. Treatment usually focuses on *psychodynamic* factors, that is, the inner structures and conflicts that contribute to the problem. One form of this approach, *psychoanalytic psychotherapy*, focuses intensively on the relationship between the patient and therapist as a sort of laboratory to understand how the patient functions. The therapist and patient embark together on the task of understanding the patient's world as fully and completely as possible. This way, the patient discovers ways to make her world a better, healthier place to live. No easy task, this thorough approach can take from months to years to accomplish.

Eclectic Psychotherapy. Many therapists have learned a variety of approaches. They may use a combination of psychodynamic, cognitive-behavioral, Gestalt, and systems theory. Knowing that eating disorders have multiple causes, they choose tools appropriate to patients' needs and stage of therapy.

Systems Theory. In this theory, the family is seen as an interlocking system, each member in balance with the others. When one person changes, the whole family reacts. Family members, however, often try to keep the same old balance, resisting change even if they know change is better for everyone in the long run. The therapist's job is to help the family change so members can grow and become independent, and can openly and honestly communicate feelings and needs. (See later section on family therapy.)

Cognitive-Behavioral Training. This approach teaches that faulty thinking patterns support eating disorders. For instance, a patient may think she is so worthless that it is not important to take the time to cook healthy meals. Or she may believe that if she gives in to her feelings, she will melt or disappear or "never get back to normal"—so she turns to food to squash down the feelings. Patients are taught how to identify and change these faulty beliefs.

Combining Treatments. In some cases, a patient may be working with several professionals, such as a psychotherapist, nutritionist, pediatrician or internist, dentist, or social worker. At first glance, this may seem excessive. But some people do need a variety of services to resolve their eating problems in a timely manner.

Group Therapy. Group therapy is conducted at hospitals and university counseling centers, and by therapists in private practice. Sometimes groups offer the best treatment for a person at a particular stage of recovery. Often, groups are used along with individual treatment. In a group, the patient can meet others who share her problem, discover that other people think she is worthwhile, test her ability to be honest, and learn new skills of communicating, sharing feelings, and coping.

Groups can address general themes common in eating disorders. Or they may have a specific focus, such as body image, parents, or careers. They may be short-term (fewer than ten sessions) or long-term.

Art Therapy. Crayons, paints, clay, or other artistic materials have been used for decades to help people in therapy. Art can help a person uncover, express, and work through feelings she previously couldn't verbalize.

> *Gwendolyn came from a family that prized harmony and the values of compassion, responsibility to feed the earth's hungry, and respect for animals. In addition to the six children in the family itself, no fewer than ten foster children passed through the household at one time or another. Family members were expected to be polite and to cooperate in managing chores. Gwen's mother became ill and was an invalid from the time Gwen was seven. As the second oldest child, and oldest girl, Gwen found herself in charge of the younger children.*
>
> *She began compulsive overeating at thirteen, gaining forty pounds that year. Feeling guilty, she tried to cure herself, with little success. Then she began vomiting, which made her even more unhappy and despondent. She was evaluated and then hospitalized on the eating disorders unit of a local hospital.*
>
> *In group therapy, she listened attentively to others' problems and seemed to comply with the treatment program—but she was not getting better. An art therapist finally got her to make*

clay sculptures of her brothers and sisters. This brought unexpected vitality, as Gwen molded and smashed the clay with gusto. The very act of making crude portraits and then destroying them was a relief. Later, she was able to make portraits and leave them long enough to serve as the focus for discussing her feelings about the family. Slowly she began to express her pain.

As a politically active gay woman, Gwen knew women's bodies are valuable and beautiful, whatever their shape. Yet this knowledge hadn't always translated into respect for her own body. As she resolved her eating disorder, Gwen could feel real acceptance for her body, a shift that also improved her relationship with her lover.

Movement Therapy. Movement therapy attempts to do with body movement what art therapy does with materials such as paints and clay. Participating in dance, yoga, and other modes of creative expression can help a patient become more self-aware and improve her body image.

Body Image and Esteem. Hatred of the body is pervasive in eating disordered people, and repairing body esteem is an essential part of treatment. The main form of this body hate is hatred of fat. This problem is intensified by body image distortion. Many people misperceive their actual size and see a normal-sized stomach as grossly fat. Body image groups help patients become aware of their feelings toward their bodies and learn healthier relationships to them. Body image work can be done in a group or in individual therapy. Art, movement, guided imagery, and verbal, insight-oriented therapy, may be used.

Family Therapy

Some professionals in the field of eating disorders believe it critical to involve the family in therapy, particularly if a patient is hospitalized. To the family, hospitalization can represent an admission of failure. It can also mean a major investment of time, money, and energy, or, at the very least, a surrender of power to strangers. Family therapy can help clarify these reactions. It can also clarify the patient's feelings about hospitalization—triumph, relief, or reluctance—that might otherwise remain unexpressed. Family therapy provides a forum for parents to express and get help with their concerns.

Family therapy is especially important if the eating disordered person is a minor or is living with the family, for the family provides the day-to-day environment that is so influential in eating disorders.

Family therapy performs three functions:

1. It tackles original family problems such as poor communication, unclear boundaries, or unrealistic expectations.
2. It lets the family know professionals see them as having an active role in the patient's recovery.
3. It helps ensure the hospitalized patient's family has a cooperative relationship with the hospital staff.

Some hospitals offer support groups for family members. These can provide information and help the family become acquainted with the people providing the care. The support group may deal with

- information about the disorders;
- feelings of isolation, mistrust, anger, and guilt;
- control issues;
- dealing with other relatives who may be intrusive, authoritarian, or perfectionistic;
- sexuality;
- the patient's personality.[1]

Kate became curious about her disorder. She wondered how it had developed. Andrea (her doctor) recommended some books, and Kate was fascinated to find out that her own discovery of vomiting out excess food had been made simultaneously by thousands of other women. She was a bit scared to read that some of them continued the habit for ten or fifteen years. Her heart sank. Could she succeed in recovering promptly when so many others had failed? Andrea noticed Kate's changed manner the next session, and asked why she seemed so worried. Kate said she was afraid she would never get well.

Andrea explained that bulimia is a disorder that is curable. In the last few years, great strides have been made in understanding and treating bulimia. Former bulimics, even though they face some obstacles and risks, can go on to lead happy lives, have children, engage in athletics, and generally do whatever they want. Andrea urged Kate to attend a lecture given by another local therapist. Kate decided to go.

There were several dozen people in attendance, of all different ages and sizes, and even some men. The speaker explained more about the different kinds of eating disorders, and then told the audience she too had had a problem. How great was Kate's surprise when this poised, assured, and knowledgeable woman said that she had been a bulimic-anorexic herself! Kate listened with a mixture of hope, disbelief, skepticism, and fascination to this therapist's story. She decided to join a Twelve Step group, a move Andrea heartily supported.

How Long Does Treatment Take?

Vera had been in treatment for two years and three days. She was discouraged and so were her parents and friends. Her boyfriend thought it was "taking forever" and urged her to drop out. Vera felt really nervous about this pressure, especially since she also doubted that the treatment was working.

Fortunately, she spoke about her doubts to her therapist, Barbara. Barbara explained that this was an opportunity for Vera to evaluate the progress she had made, and to check whether she had any unspoken reluctance to be done with her symptom and to say goodbye to therapy. Together, Vera and Barbara reviewed the two years. They noted that, in that time, Vera had stopped taking care of everyone in sight and now concentrated more on her own needs. She had learned to drive, made new

*friends, and found a job she liked. They chuckled as they re-
called a few false starts Vera had made in unpleasant jobs,
times she had really needed Barbara's support. She had also
stopped being so hard on herself, and begun to believe she was
a worthwhile person.*

*When she realized how far she had come, Vera was much
relieved. Her self-confidence improved even more, and she now
felt ready to tackle the last remaining problem—the original
symptom, her bingeing.*

Therapy may deal very successfully with some aspects of the
eating disorder, but "results" may not yet be apparent. Don't be
disheartened if you don't see immediate change. Often, small,
internal changes precede big, external ones. Long before you
see results, therapy will be dealing with self-esteem, communication skills, and assertion. It can take time for trust to develop so that the therapist knows the true extent of the problem
and can develop and implement a full treatment plan. It takes
time to create new habits.

One factor influencing the length of treatment is when, in
the course of her illness, the person came in for therapy. Has
she been bingeing and purging for twenty years, or for three
months? Is anorexia advanced, or something she began showing signs of last summer? Generally, the sooner the person
seeks help with the problem, the easier it is to overcome. If it is
less entrenched, fewer behaviors that compensate for the problem have grown up around it, and "normal" life is not that far
in the past.

By contrast, a person whose disorder goes back many years
may have a longer struggle. But this is not a hard and fast rule.
Some people have, on their own, done a lot of inner searching
and skill-building, and have already gained important tools by
the time they begin therapy. And we must acknowledge, as
therapists, that even professionals cannot predict with accuracy
who will improve quickly, and who will struggle.

Have patience with the recovering person. Being in therapy can be very hard work. Part of the challenge can be the very act of sticking with it through times of discouragement. This can be the forerunner of a renewed sense of commitment which the recovering person can take to future projects.

The Rhythm of Recovery: Progress and Relapses

Lynne and Zelda both had bulimia. They attended a reputable clinic that offered medical supervision, psychotherapy, behavioral techniques, and nutritional counseling. Lynne's progress was visible from the start, but Zelda had to work harder to make headway against her disorder.

After three months, both were doing much better. Their bingeing and purging habits were well in hand. Then one day it happened. Zelda's old boyfriend came to town, and when she saw him with another woman, Zelda locked herself in her apartment and binged for an hour. Soon her habit seemed as bad as ever.

Recovery rarely takes a perfectly smooth path. Progress may be interspersed with setbacks, and a relapse does not necessarily mean that treatment has failed. Some relapses are triggered by stressful events. Others happen because the client is testing her ability in a greater variety of situations and has met one she has not quite mastered.

A relapse can be a measure of growth. It reveals the contrast between the old problem and the new lifestyle the client has learned. Thus, it is important not to panic unnecessarily if a setback occurs.

It can be a delicate task, however, to distinguish between legitimately excusing a minor slip, and making rationalizations for remaining ill. Both you and the recovering person need to know that the occasional lapse does not mean, "All is lost; start over from the beginning." It is the *commitment* to work toward recovery which should be uninterrupted.

Some people can change their eating (or purging) behavior relatively soon in therapy, and then spend time examining the origins of their problem. Others seem to have to work out all the sources and meanings first. The eating symptom may be the last thing to go. The three graphs that follow show you some different patterns of recovery.

Lynne had been bingeing and purging three times a day, and soon after she began therapy, this frequency went way down. She had a bit of a plateau, and then she progressed further.

Lynne's Progress

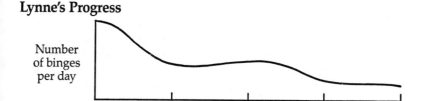

Zelda also had been bingeing and purging three times a day. But her frequency declined much more slowly and gradually.

Zelda's Progress

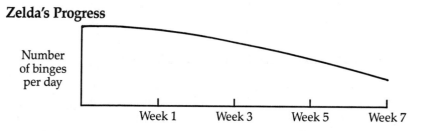

A third patient, whom we'll call Carla, had yet a different pattern. She experienced a dramatic relief in the beginning, but then had a reverse and went back to her initial frequency. Then renewed progress occurred, followed by a gradual decline in frequency. One more "blip" in her graph was followed by ulti-mate full recovery.

Carla's Progress

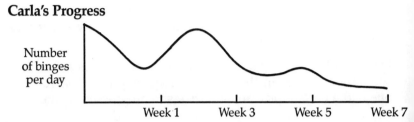

Number
of binges
per day

Week 1   Week 3   Week 5   Week 7

For some, therapy is a six-month experience requiring one session a week. For others, it may take several years at twice (or more times) a week. Still others need the resources of a hospital program. Each person can only work at her own pace and the one who needs more time in therapy is not necessarily more disturbed. An otherwise bright, active, and productive person may have a persistent eating disorder—rather like a nagging knee injury that seems to take forever to heal—while going about a nearly normal life.

If a slip occurs after a patient is no longer in therapy, a few "booster" sessions or the resumption of therapy for a while may be in order.

When Therapy Doesn't Seem to be Helping

Occasionally, therapy can seem unhelpful, even when prog-ress is being made. The truth often hurts. Therapy is not fun, and a person who is working on problems can be in consider-able discomfort. At such times, the therapy can become a target for blame. Giving up a familiar, all-purpose solution to life's problems is difficult for anyone.

But there may be good reason to question therapy. The treat-ment method may not be appropriate for a particular person. If the patient senses such a mismatch, she should discuss it honestly with the therapist so, working together, they can find a solution.

After a fair trial of three to ten sessions the patient may conclude that the therapist is not right for her. Whether the mismatch is due to poor rapport, error, or miscommunication, moving on to another therapist may be the best move. A good therapist will help in the search.

> *Eleanor was not satisfied in her therapy with Meg. Eleanor's physician had referred her to Meg, whose credentials were impeccable. Although they tried to work through Eleanor's dissatisfaction, the feeling of a poor "fit" would not go away. Finally, Meg suggested that Eleanor might do better with another therapist and suggested three people to contact.*
>
> *Eleanor spoke with all three on the phone and made an appointment with Robert. They hit it off at once, and she felt able to confide her deepest feelings and fears. It turned out that this was what she had needed more than the practical guidance Meg offered. With Robert's help, Eleanor traced her eating problem back to her past, specifically to the time her father was killed when she was eight. She also felt that seeing a male therapist might help her better understand her reactions to men.*
>
> *Sandra, on the other hand, had changed therapists three times in eight months when she first met Annette, her new therapist. The first thing they worked on was Sandra's desire to quit. This desire typically appeared whenever Sandra felt too uncomfortable with another person. This habit had created problems in her personal life, and working on it in therapy helped her avoid further losses of friendships. Soon Sandra and Annette had cleared the way for work on the eating problem to take place.*

Evaluating Group Therapy's Usefulness. Is group therapy useful to every person with an eating disorder? We know that it helps many. But eating disorder therapy groups can have high drop-out rates. This probably reflects resistance to the special challenges involved in revealing one's innermost thoughts in a setting which is less private than the one-to-one encounter with a sympathetic therapist. Some patients need the undivided attention of individual therapy and find group therapy less useful. For others, individual therapy is most important, with group therapy a useful adjunct. The therapist and patient together should evaluate the need for group therapy.

Patients often experience *resistance* to therapy, a kind of self-imposed pushing away from treatment. Some patients leave group because they are too resistant to work effectively there. Resistance can stem from a real fear of revealing one's inner self and private behavior to others, a feeling of being different, or a difficulty in accepting differences between people. It is hard to know whether to press the potential dropouts to overcome their resistance. Often, if they make the effort, they find their fears can be worked through and they can begin using the group to help solve their problems. On the other hand, people who drop out of a group may just not be ready for this method. They may do better in a one-to-one setting. Those not ready for group work should not be pressured into it.

What if the Therapist Is Not an Eating Disorder Specialist? Patients sometimes work with a therapist who is not an eating disorder specialist. They may have originally begun therapy for other reasons and didn't mention their eating disorder. The treatment for the original problem may have gone quite well. But the therapist is not equipped to deal with an eating disorder. In this case, starting anew with an eating disorder specialist is quite appropriate and not a sign of failure.

Another scenario may unfold. If the present (nonspecialist) therapist has a very strong relationship with the patient and a change would set the patient back, an eating disorder specialist can be brought in as a consultant. A third way to address the eating disorder without interfering with an established therapy is to encourage the patient to join an eating disorder group.

Changing Therapists Is Sometimes Helpful. Perhaps your eating disordered friend has chosen a therapist whose technique, although effective with some patients, does not fit your friend's needs. The therapist's orientation is not "wrong," but just not the best for your friend's unique personality and needs. A change to a different therapist is justified here.

Finally, the therapist's personality may be a bad match for a particular patient. Nobody is at fault here, but the situation should be discussed openly with the practitioner. Remember, even the most talented therapist may not have that special rapport with a particular person.

But Changing Therapists Is Not Always Helpful. If, after a change of therapists, the patient still does not settle down to work on her problem, something is going on that should be examined. This may be a fear of, or shame at, needing help. Or it may stem from parental disapproval, or distrust of treatment may be interfering. At this point, it is wise to stay in therapy with the current therapist, rather than to run to yet another practitioner and start over again.

Therapists are human and make mistakes:

- A hospital treatment team (consisting of therapist, nurses, nutritionist, and medical doctor) can occasionally let an important piece of information "fall through the cracks."
- A therapist might underestimate the importance of calling a family consultation at a crucial time.
- A patient may feel abandoned by a psychiatrist who prescribes medication without explaining why.
- A group may turn out to be ineffective because the other members are older, more troubled (or less) than the patient, or unwelcoming.

In most instances, none of these examples constitutes a serious enough error to leave the therapist or the treatment unit. Changing therapists in such circumstances, if the program is otherwise functioning well, might delay the patient's progress.

Changing would also prevent the patient from learning that errors can be recognized and repaired.

Some therapeutic errors, however, justify a change. An approach that singles out only one aspect of the eating disorder for treatment—for example, family therapy only, while neglecting habit control, faulty beliefs, and nutritional evaluation—can fail by attempting too little.

If the therapy the patient undergoes is part of a research project, she may not receive help tailored to her exact needs. Researchers test one technique at a time to discover which one causes which effect. She should be thoroughly informed of research conditions beforehand. That way, she can decide if her needs will be served by participating in the study.

Finally, some patients are hard to work with. They are resistant, skeptical, or, frankly deceitful. They may cancel one session after another. Or they come late or pay erratically. They don't respond to ideas being offered, and some of them criticize and complain. Therapists get discouraged too!

Is She Recovered Yet?

We have listed below some of the problems that comprise eating disorders, and some of the landmarks that are seen in recovery. Not everyone will experience all of these, but the list can show the kinds of changes that occur.

When the eating disorder is at its worst, the eating disordered person may

- feel out of control;
- binge or purge;
- have uncomfortable weight fluctuations;
- experience physical side effects;
- look depressed, despairing;
- make poor food choices, eating junk foods or only one kind of food instead of a variety of healthful foods;
- organize life around food or restriction of food;

- have tenuous or limited relationships;
- deny the existence of a problem.

As recovery begins the eating disordered person may

- be in control a little more of the time;
- be bingeing and purging less or with less self-hate;
- have less extreme weight fluctuations;
- have some physical symptoms decrease in severity or disappear;
- seem less depressed;
- make better food choices;
- have more time for other pursuits and thoughts;
- put more energy into relationships;
- seem better at times, and just as bad as ever at other times;
- tell you that she is working on a problem.

Significant progress has been made when

- bingeing and purging are reduced greatly;
- she seems to like and respect herself more;
- she relates to people more fully, seeming to be more genuinely interested in others;
- she seems less depressed and can explain how she copes with and manages her feelings more constructively;
- she improves her food choices and seems to be eating (and digesting) more healthful foods;
- her weight shows even less fluctuation;
- physical side effects seem less pronounced and she complains less of them;
- she can tell you about the various psychological problems she is working on and what she has been doing to solve them.

In the final stages of recovery the eating disordered person

- seems to think well of herself;
- seems proud of how she handles herself, her feelings, her decision-making, and life in general;

- can cope with life's stresses most of the time without binge-ing, purging, or restricting;
- can describe what situations make her feel bad and what she can do about them;
- can fully admit she had a problem and can tell you what she has done about it.

If therapy has been primarily symptom-focused, it can now conclude. Symptom management, however, may have been but one goal in a therapy designed to help a person identify and deal with underlying issues such as low self-esteem, a repeated pattern of destructive relationships, or fear of success. Then treatment may continue even after symptoms have disappeared and mood has improved.

> *Kate had now been in treatment for two months. In her individual sessions she had let down her facade and begun to get to know the inner self she had been running from. She realized how little she trusted anyone—including Andrea—and how much of her life had been lived to please and impress others. And now, in group, she was meeting others with the same problem, and finding that she was accepted in spite of her secret!*
>
> *Then came a crisis. Her youngest brother was injured in a car accident. And, worse, he had been drinking at the time. Kate couldn't believe he had started drinking again, and she practically yelled at him on the phone. All at once, Kate's old fears came back in a rush. She would have to catch a flight back to her hometown, visit the critical care unit, apologize for her outburst, comfort her frantic mother—the whole prospect was awful. Suddenly, it didn't seem so wonderful to have all her inner life so exposed. That old numbness seemed kind of inviting. Kate began to fantasize about bingeing.*
>
> *And one night she did it: she brought home a gallon of ice cream and a pie, ate them all, and threw up. The next day she felt dreadful. How could she face Andrea, looking and feeling like this? She cancelled her therapy appointment and binged*

and purged all day. When the telephone rang, she somehow knew who it would be, and was terrified at being found out in this terrible state. Andrea asked what was the matter. Bursting into tears, Kate explained what had happened. She felt like such a failure—burdened with this family trauma, and now Andrea was going to be mad at her, or maybe she'd decide she wouldn't work with Kate anymore. Kate could hardly believe it when Andrea was nice and asked what she could do to help. Kate gladly accepted the offer of an emergency session the next day. She was so relieved she was even able to go out to a movie that evening.

By morning, Kate was sure it had been a mistake to accept the appointment, but for some reason she went anyway. It would have been too gross to stand Andrea up twice. Full of dread, Kate arrived. Surely, Andrea would be disgusted! Kate had backslid. She had shouted at her brother. She had missed an appointment, and then bawled like a baby over the telephone. She had never felt so embarrassed in her life!

Andrea began the session by listening carefully and assuring Kate that what Kate had done illustrated how normal feelings get translated into bingeing behavior. On receiving the phone call about the car accident, Kate had been frightened, angry, worried—and at this great distance from her brother, unable to do anything to help. A surge of emotions had nowhere to go—the binge and purge was the only outlet she had. Kate would never again wonder if all this talk about the inner drama was really related to her weird eating—now she knew!

Then Andrea lightened the tone by telling about a time when she was so upset she absentmindedly brushed her teeth with Ben-Gay. Kate couldn't help giggling at this and pretty soon she began to realize that people do get upset and they survive. Together, Kate and Andrea prepared for Kate's upcoming trip, clarifying what she expected from each family member, how to explain her therapy, and how to handle the unexpected.

CHAPTER 9

Hospitalization

Hospitalization may be needed in a medical or psychiatric crisis: the patient may be fainting, starving, threatening suicide, or unable to manage independently. On the other hand, hospitalization may represent a carefully chosen step in recovery. The person may be functioning well but need an intensive, all-around approach to uproot an entrenched eating problem. In either case, the hospital eating disorder unit offers the support of special therapies (art, music, movement, vocational, occupational), a community of peers, and nutritional supervision, in addition to medical care and psychotherapy. Used together, these resources can help speed the patient's recovery.

Anorexics may be hospitalized when they have significant weight loss, malnourishment, severely depressed moods, or thoughts or intentions of suicide. Other factors that may favor hospitalization are failure to respond to outpatient treatment, a family overwhelmed by the problem or who seem to be contributing to it, or a lack of adequate outpatient care in the area.

Bulimics should consider hospitalization for similar reasons, especially if eating or purging behavior feels out of control despite outpatient therapy. Use of Ipecac, a life crisis (losing a job or an important relationship), stealing, drug use, or other forms of self-harm all make hospitalization something for bulimics to consider.

Marcie didn't understand why everyone was so concerned. She felt fine! Her work as a fund-raiser interested her, she had her own apartment, and she never had to worry about her weight. She just put food out of her mind. That was so much easier than dieting, with all its measuring and counting. But her sleep was shallow and unrestful, and her concentration was poor. She resented friends' pleading with her to eat more. Stress fractures in her weakened bones interfered with the running she loved. None of these problems seemed serious enough to warrant intense treatment, and yet together they showed that her body was in poor condition.

Marcie was hospitalized for four weeks. After discharge, she said, "I didn't really want to go in, but now I see I needed it. I didn't know what was normal to eat; I kept kidding myself that I was eating enough or that I could get well by myself. But in the hospital, seeing all the other people tell similar stories, it made me think. Now I feel normal again. My exercise program is fun, not work. I'm proud of myself, and people are always complimenting me on how good I look."

Zachary, Tina, and Kyra all benefited from hospital stays, but for different reasons.

Zachary was a nineteen-year-old with everything to look forward to. A brilliant student who loved his major of engineering, he was risking it all by not eating. The trouble was, he felt fat and was terrified of gaining weight. He remembered the merciless teasing other kids had given him for being fat. At seventeen, he vowed never to be teased again. He was strict at the table, and talked very little, as if he were already imagining his new body. He buckled down to study as a way of flexing another kind of power, and surged forward in the last two years of high school. But now he was in trouble. He sometimes felt light-headed, and had mysterious chest pains.

Zachary thought hospitalization was the last thing he wanted, even though his weight was precariously low. But his doctor finally persuaded him to check in. Once there, away from his worries and distractions, Zachary faced his eating disorder for the first time. Later, he realized that admitting he was anorexic was just as crucial to his recovery as the fifteen pounds of weight he gained. Two months later, after he was out of medical danger and discharged from the hospital, he made a commitment to attend weekly individual therapy sessions and regular meetings of Overeaters Anonymous.

Tina was bulimic, and her progress was frustratingly slow. Moreover, Tina wanted to explore body image problems more thoroughly than could be done in an outpatient setting. She decided to take her annual vacation and some sick leave from work to participate in an inpatient program for one month. This helped her go three entire weeks without purging. What a difference that made! Now she knew firsthand what a healthy body and normal eating and thinking patterns felt like. She learned how a person can relate to others without fear and guilt. This way, she got the incentive needed to continue her recovery at home.

Kyra felt overwhelmed grappling with her compulsive overeating, and was barely able to get through the day. For her, the hospital was a place to get away from worldly responsibilities long enough to change the way she thought about food. It was a relief to escape her sense of isolation. Choosing hospitalization was a clear decision in favor of life.

Choosing the Hospital

The best eating disorder units have a clear, consistent philosophy of treatment. The program should be well-rounded, including services such as family therapy, body-image work, art and movement therapy, individual and group therapy, and nutrition and medical supervision. Ask to talk with the program coordinator, who can tell you about staff background, training, and credentials. Read the brochures. Your family doctor may be able to add key information to help you make your choice. If a therapist is already in the picture, his or her recommendation is valuable.

Eating disorder units are typically small, with four to eight beds. The staff will include doctors, therapists, nutritionists, and those very important people, the nurses, whose care and expertise are such a vital part of a hospital unit's effectiveness.

Hospital personnel conduct the initial interview to assess whether a hospital stay is in the patient's best interest. Methods of financing the stay are also investigated. This interview should give you some idea of the length of stay and its cost. In the San Francisco Bay Area where we work, most eating disorder units expect patients to stay four to six weeks, or in some cases as long as three months. For some patients, repeated hospitalizations (brief or extended) are useful as they struggle to take care of themselves in healthful ways. Some hospitals make Overeaters Anonymous and the Twelve Step approach an integral part of the hospitalization, even hosting meetings on site.

Each patient's path to recovery is unique. Good hospital programs recognize this and help the patient use her own and community resources to get better.

The Hospital Stay

There are several parts to a hospital stay. First, the patient is stabilized if her health is in danger. This may involve giving her nutritional supplements or potassium injections. Second, the patient learns about healthy nutrition and eating styles to make sure that the cure is lasting. This occurs through a requirement to eat whatever food is on the tray. One of the strongest features of the hospital program, which distinguishes it from other forms of treatment, is intensive monitoring of eating and eliminating. The patient will not be allowed to binge, purge, or starve. Naturally, taking away these familiar coping strategies means other, healthful strategies will need to be adopted to fill the void.

The patient's body is monitored through medical tests that evaluate blood chemistry and organ functions. Each hospital program has special aspects that may include dance or movement therapy, art classes, cooking lessons, and clothes shopping. Each also deals with a patient's thinking around food through individual, group, and family therapy sessions.

The patient may go through several stages during a hospital stay, each with its challenges. At admission there is much to adjust to, and the patient and family may experience many feelings, from relief to resentment. Then the all-day program is begun. The patient must adjust to learning from many people: nurses, doctors, nutritionists, and teachers. That's a lot of people to let into your life at one time!

As treatment takes hold and the disorder loosens its grip, different reactions may occur. Anorexics, for example, may feel panic as their weight rises to near normal. And completing the hospital stay calls for the person to prepare for a new lifestyle outside, to say good-bye to the people she met in the hospital, and to see herself in a new way.

Feelings: Hers and Yours

The patient may arrive on the unit unwilling, doubtful, or mistakenly confident of an effortless, miracle cure. Probably she feels a mixture of relief and resentment—relief at having others take control and provide structure; resentment over losing autonomy and needing to be in the hospital. Whatever her initial outlook, it can be expected to change a number of times during her stay. If she has been hospitalized before, it may take a special effort to overcome the pessimism she may be feeling.

It is natural for the patient to be restless in an environment where everything, including the most intimate bodily functions, will be observed and recorded. Her food will be chosen, her eating watched, bathroom stays monitored, and the days fully scheduled. She will probably dislike some of the rules. But it is important that you not mistake her complaints for a sound judgment that the program is "bad." The complaints may actually be a way of declaring some measure of independence, of asking for sympathy, or of making conversation. Or she may be flexing new assertiveness muscles or minimizing the fact that hospitalization is useful. Nurses in a hospital unit we visited recently reported that eating disorder patients often threaten to leave the unit, but seldom do.

A subtler discontent may spring from the threat of losing her main way of coping with life: the distorted eating pattern. Facing life without it is a challenge, requiring all the support that staff and other patients on the unit can give.

Your feelings about her hospitalization are noticed. If you support her presence, that is one less thing for her to worry about. But if you don't support treatment, the easier it will be for her to manipulate the situation and defeat the treatment.

Thinking In Extremes

Many patients with eating disorders see things in extremes. They see the world in black and white, putting the good in one corner and the bad in another. This extreme thinking comes into play both in and out of the hospital.

> *Tina told the hospital staff that the therapist she had been seeing in the community was not at all useful, but the hospital staff members were great—just completely wonderful. Also, her parents were "the best parents in the world" and could do no wrong. This outpatient therapist was the only problem.*

> *Kyra, on the other hand, hated her parents, saying they were dreadful in every way. She also vehemently hated the attending psychiatrist, but idolized the head nurse and the nutritionist.*

Professionals are trained to help the patient see such extreme characterizations of people. They are aware of patients' tendencies to cast people as angels and devils, reflecting an inner division between the patients' own "good" and "bad" sides.

One potential hazard of this extreme thinking is that significant others can get drawn into the situation and end up fighting among themselves. In essence, they are joining in the patient's inner battle.

What can the family do? First, understand what is going on behind the scenes. Remember that extreme thinking creates painful situations for her and for others. Also, you can help by being aware of this situation and not endorsing "villain" and "angel" views of hospital and professional staffs. In other words, if your daughter tells you that she hates her therapist and wants to work only with the nutritionist, encourage her to discuss the situation with her therapist. She may need to learn more about her extreme thinking, and the hospital is an excellent place to do this.

You will probably have to cope with unsettling feelings of your own. You may feel threatened. Turning a loved one over to a team of strangers who suddenly seem closer to her than you are may cause jealousy and fear. You might end up thinking, *Maybe she won't need me so much! Maybe she's telling them bad things about me!*

Some people dread having strangers know their secrets or a family "weakness." Others may also resent the cost of the stay. Often, the unhappiness felt by family members or significant others arises from loss of control and a sense of failure. "We tried so hard . . . and now this." Even if you know objectively that you have done your best, feelings of failure can arise.

On the other hand, you may harbor a guilty pleasure in being relieved of his or her management. No more locked cupboards, no more anguished mealtimes, no more bathroom conflicts, more time for the other children or friends. Try not to feel guilty about this. The time she spends in a hospital can serve as a time of rest and introspection for you.

Take advantage of services the hospital offers to help you work through your own and other family members' emotional issues as they relate to the patient. You can help by facing your feelings, just as she must face hers. Indeed, it may be the most helpful thing you can do. It's a way to learn about hardships she may have been imposing on people, such as taking their food or giving them cause for anxiety. Some units believe in family involvement so strongly that they require the family's participation in therapy before they will admit a patient.

Day Treatment

Some hospitals now have inpatient day treatment programs for their newly discharged patients. That is, the patient spends much of each day at the hospital, but goes home to sleep. These patients may have graduated from full inpatient treatment, but are not yet ready to manage on only one or two hours a week of outpatient treatment. Other patients in day treatment have not required hospitalization, but need more than individual therapy. These day programs provide structured mealtimes, nutritional and medical monitoring, and therapeutic activities such as art therapy, body-image group, and individual or group therapy. In addition, many hospitals now offer free support groups for former and current patients. These groups can make life easier for the person who has left the hospital.

Aftercare

It may be tempting to hope that hospitalization will solve the problem once and for all. But this is unrealistic. The world with its conflicts and temptations will still be there. Family and friends will not have changed overnight. After a person leaves a hospital, she is usually encouraged to begin or continue outpatient therapy. This further treatment will help her to stabilize her gains as she reenters and faces the pressures and temptations of her world, integrating good habits such as appropriate food choice and healthier ways to see herself and the world. Aftercare also provides a place for the person to work through the many underlying issues that may have caused the eating disorder. We want to emphasize that hospitalization is an aid in certain cases, not a cure-all.

CHAPTER 10

You and Your Needs

Family and friends often need to know their role in the eating disorder problem. They may ask themselves, *Am I responsible for my loved one's disorder?* The word *responsible* has two meanings: on one hand, it implies guilt or blame, that uneasy feeling of past wrongdoing, and on the other, it suggests an opportunity for here-and-now, positive action.

Did I Help Cause the Problem?

Let's remember what we know about causes. Eating disorders are created by the interaction of many things: the patient's personality, the culture, and the biology of dieting. The family is also one of the influences at play.

Family members exert pressures on each other. Children tease each other about all kinds of things, including the way they look. Parents sometimes maintain standards that children may feel helpless to live up to. Significant others may insult and injure each other, sometimes unintentionally, sometimes purposefully.

There are several ways a family can contribute to a person's eating disorder.

1. Good Intentions... For Whose Benefit?

Even good intentions may go awry. A mother, perhaps reliving or regretting her youthful days, may insist that her daughter have a perfect figure. A father, intending to build character, may impose impossible standards of perfection on his children, frowning when they bring home report cards with B's on them and expecting them to feel and act in a way that makes *him* feel important.

2. Forgetting the Child's Needs

The admirable qualities of the patient-to-be may play a part. Let's say one child in the family has serious problems—an illness, learning disability, or alcohol dependency. The parents are preoccupied with this needy child. The patient-to-be decides to shoulder some of the burden, to be strong, not needy, perfect. This allows the parents to take him or her for granted: "She's such a good girl, never gives us any trouble." Or, "Johnny is remarkable for a twelve-year-old—so helpful, a godsend." But this child, too, has needs.

3. Using Others to Fill Our Needs

We sometimes want other people to be a certain way, so we won't have to feel certain "bad" things.

- "Love me so I won't feel lonely."
- "Let me be helpless with my illness so I won't have to grow up."
- "Be as ladylike as I am so I won't have to be annoyed, because I can't handle my annoyance appropriately."
- "Be a success so I can bask in reflected glory."
- "Be a success so people will praise my parenting."

This common and very human process means we are using other people to fill our needs. We all do this to some extent. But when their needs differ from ours, and we go on trying to overrule them and impose our needs, this becomes exploitation. This is how one person contributes to the other person's illness, be it compulsive eating, gambling, or anything else. You may have contributed to an eating disorder if you *required* a person to be smart, attractive, a caretaker, a go-between, or the okay kid in the family. If, for instance, you need your daughter to get straight A's every semester because you feel unsure about your own success, you can help her and yourself by taking a longer look at your need for success. Then try to meet that need yourself, for yourself.

It is more ominous when we use others in ways that hurt them.

- "Don't succeed. I would feel inferior."
- "Gee, it's too bad you have a problem, but at least it takes the spotlight off me."
- "If you're fat, I won't have to feel jealous."
- "I don't like your drinking, but I can stand it—in fact, I wouldn't know what to do with a happy relationship."
- "Be mean to me, so my suffering pays off my sins."

By honestly examining our relationships, we may find such hidden wishes as these. This is a good time to discuss them frankly and openly. A counselor can help in the discussion, if it seems too much to handle on your own. Such unfriendly wishes, when they are traced to the source, almost always spring from thwarted natural needs—such as a wish for esteem. Admitting them does not mean you are a bad person, but that you have uncovered a need. We invite you to strive to meet that original need directly, not through someone else's discomfort.

4. Not Acknowledging Someone's Feelings

A fourth way families can promote an eating disorder is by ignoring the distress of one family member. Many people cannot stand to see the tears of sadness, or the shudders of fear. They will do almost anything to avoid seeing such feelings. They may be overwhelmed already, or they may simply not know how to handle uncomfortable emotions.

If someone they care about is in distress, or is feeling anger or disappointment, they say something like, "Don't cry," "Toughen up," or "Look how lucky you are in this world of wars and refugees." They may even leave the room. These people "help" by hurrying the sufferer to get the suffering over with to lessen their own discomfort. The sufferer, however, may just need to cry and learn to handle feelings, not to hide them more effectively. Many an eating disordered person has buried her feelings with food to protect another family member from having to deal with them.

From such family responses to fear, anger, and disappointment, the eating disordered person learns she must squelch her feelings. Food is one way she finds to do this. She gradually loses track of where one person's life ends and another's begins. The sufferer may misinterpret the message, "Mom can't handle your pain" as

• "No one cares."
• "I'm no good."
• "I mustn't cry, or Mom won't love me."

In treatment she learns her feelings are hers and she is entitled to them, and that other people's feelings are theirs, and not her responsibility.

In investigating your role in the eating disorder, you should know that therapists don't use the term "blame." For one thing, blame punishes without solving, making people feel bad. Naturally, this tempts those who are blamed to avoid the subject and delay dealing with the present feelings. It stops the process of healing.

How You Can Make the Right Choices

Family members do play a part in the problem. You did "this" when you could have done "that." Though you did it your way for good reasons that made sense at the time, you chose a certain path and that path had certain effects. When the history of your loved one's eating disorder is written, there may well be a paragraph about how "Dad insisted I get good grades," or "My brothers always teased me about being chubby."

Yet there is a balance of responsibility between you and the patient, for at each moment we have a choice. Suppose you teased your sister about fat. She had a choice of what to do: she could have ignored you, teased you back, overruled your remark by boasting about something else, spit in your eye, or complained about you to a friend. Or she could have felt wounded and tried to make sure the teasing never happened again by dieting rigidly or becoming an expert people-pleaser. A young woman who develops an eating disorder tends to choose the last-named option: believing the criticism, believing the other person has a right to criticize, and believing she must remove the cause for criticism.

In her therapy, however, she is learning—or rather, being reminded — that she did have other options, ones that would not have led down the path to eating disorders.

You have probably also thought you had no choice in a particular situation when really you did. Perhaps you thought, *I couldn't have possibly let the neighbors know we're not perfect, or left my husband (even though he's a practicing alcoholic), or told my co-worker I didn't approve of her stealing supplies.* In reality you *did* have the choice to let the neighbors see the truth, or reevaluate your marriage, or to stand up for your values. Now, as you look back, you have the opportunity to make new choices.

It is important to distinguish between your real responsibility to the eating disordered person, and a sense of guilt over contributing to the problem. If you have in some way contributed to the problem, changing your behavior—or making a special effort by coming to therapy, if invited, and encouraging her growth—is appropriate. Perhaps this means attending family therapy sessions or trying to communicate more honestly. No one, however, can relive the past. Recovery means that she accepts responsibility for her life and you for yours.

It is helpful for you to remain caring but not guilt-ridden. Once you have (perhaps with a therapist's help) reviewed your role in the matter, don't overstep and act as if her problem is your problem. We have seen many well-intentioned parents call repeatedly to therapists or hospital units, never really letting daughters take over their own recovery. Distinguish between your need to help and her need to be helped. In the long run, you will both benefit from her accepting responsibility for her life.

Entanglement

Entanglement means that one person worries so much about the other person's life that it almost seems they are the same person. It's easy to become entangled in another person's problems, especially if you care about him or her—but it is not healthy for either person.

For example, a mother may hover over her youngest child, long after that child is grown, because the mother needs to "be in the mother role." She might unwittingly handicap her youngest child's natural growth toward independence.

Or a father may interfere in a child's therapy, reading a lot of books, asking the therapist or hospital team lots of questions, gaining knowledge, and trying to act in a therapeutic way— because he needs to demonstrate mastery and expertise. Instead, his real contribution is not to be another therapist but to be the best, most honest father he can be.

These roles may be reversed: there are fathers dependent on their children's need for them, and underinvolved mothers. But in either case, entanglement creates an inability to determine where one person's life ends and another begins. For example, some people with eating disorders feel overly responsible for others. They hide their problems and feelings and tiptoe around emotions for fear of causing the slightest inconvenience to another. They really believe they are responsible for another person's every moment of happiness. This is unnecessary and may be part of the problem.

Arthur had always seen himself as a nice boy. As a child he was fat and was teased mercilessly. As an adolescent, he began acting like a Cheshire cat—mysterious, always smiling, and likely to disappear without warning. But he never imposed his feelings on anyone—especially his mother, who was working

> *at two jobs so that she could send extra money to her own ailing mother. Inside, he felt horrible. The more he hid his feelings, to protect others, the worse he felt. By the time he was nineteen, all he was in touch with was the desire to binge and purge. In therapy, Arthur had to relearn the boundaries between himself and other people—that he really did have a right to his feelings and to ask his mother for help.*

On the other hand, sometimes an eating disordered child rules the house, and it is the parents who "walk on eggs," as if afraid that the least expression of their needs will send their daughter to the hospital. This creates an intoxicating and scary situation for a young person. She may have too much control over others. We know of one family so terrorized by the daughter's eating disorder that while they were all watching television she would lean over and vomit into the wastebasket while they sat frozen in fear.[1] It can help for family or household members to recover their balance concerning their needs about such things as normal mealtimes, bedtimes, and family responsibilities.

Are You Entangled in the Problem?

Here are questions that might help you discover if you are entangled in her problem:

- Do you criticize her body or endorse the fashionably thin image?
- Do you spend too much time reassuring her?
- Do you encourage her to eat when she is not hungry?
- Do you talk a lot about food, figures, and dieting?
- Do you get overinvolved with her diet attempts, agreeing to lock the refrigerator, or otherwise becoming an "assistant food manager"? Is the family's meal pattern focused around her (time, place, menu, mood, topics of conversation)?
- Do you "innocently" offer foods that are fattening or otherwise difficult for her to deal with?
- Do you try to lose weight with her? Do you gain when she is losing or lose when she is gaining?

If you are entangled with the eating disordered person's problem, it is wise to step back. Remember your long-standing "regular" relationship with the person. Concern about the problem is just one part of the larger scene.

Here are practical guidelines to put your relationships in proper perspective:

1. *Eat the way you wish, enjoying foods you like in your own way.* Be yourself when it comes to quantities, nutritional choices, and speed of eating.
2. *Don't bow to her needs, but don't ignore them either.* Negotiate kitchen and meal arrangements just as you would other areas of life, with some concern for the other person and some for yourself.
3. *Remember the positive aspects of her body and yours.* Fat or thin, tall or short, bodies are to be accepted and enjoyed. This is extremely important for her to learn. She may forget that her body also has skills—typing, skating, playing a musical instrument — and that it is capable of nonfood pleasures.
4. *Be honest about your feelings.* If you have given all the sympathetic support you can, and are tired of listening to comments about food or body, say so. You can convey these messages as "I" statements:

   - "I'm not willing to hear more food talk just now."
   - "I've reached my limit on this topic."

5. *If you have a problem with food or body image, consider seeking help for yourself.* Now might be a good time to get help. Sometimes the pain of another person can tune us in to our own.

Codependency

Codependency, another problematic relationship style, is more than entanglement. It means actually getting something from the person having a problem (for example, deriving a sense of importance from taking care of someone who appears to be in need).

Codependency (also called *enabling*), has been found among friends and family members of problem drinkers. Codependents cover up drinkers' absences and hangovers, purchase their alcohol, and excuse their irresponsible behavior. In doing so, they gain feelings of importance and usefulness, while the alcoholic gets worse and worse.

Codependency in eating disorders works the same way. The codependent may supply the patient with forbidden food, lie to cover up embarrassing incidents, suppress his or her own legitimate needs and then feel martyred, or exert pressure on the eating disordered person to have a perfect figure. The codependent profits somehow by having attention diverted from his or her own problems to those of the person with an eating disorder.

A particularly vexing version is when the codependent becomes the watchdog over food supplies, a sort of police officer over the person's habit. This may convince the person that she is indeed too weak to solve the problem herself. Such "unhelpful help" can keep a person from growing up, while the relative feels burdened by an "immature" child or mate. Codependents rarely realize that, consciously intending only the best, they are caught up in the eating disorder too.

> *Tim unwittingly helped his wife, Maria, to stay bulimic. At first, he kept her favorite binge foods around. When she said this was a problem for her, he got rid of them. At her request, he even devised a way to lock the refrigerator. She then discovered the lock's combination and broke into the refrigerator. Then, pleading with him to help her set limits, she asked him to get a new lock, which he did.*
>
> *Maria would also leave the table in the middle of meals at restaurants to throw up. Tim concealed the fact that he found this behavior repugnant. Telling himself he was being noble and unselfish, he tolerated something he didn't like, rather than*

*confronting her. He loved Maria and thought this was the best
way to show it.*

*Unfortunately, Tim was compounding Maria's problem. She
was learning that she could rope others into her unhealthy
lifestyle, that she could avoid the consequences of her bulimia,
that she could blame him for her inability to stop purging.*

You can help yourself and the eating disordered person by
thoughtfully defining your limits and sticking to them. Your
needs and limits are legitimate, as are your worries and uncertainties. The best thing you can do for the eating disordered
person (and yourself) is to maintain yourself as a separate person,

- understanding the disorder but neither rejecting the person
  nor getting overinvolved,
- recognizing your own needs, and
- being a solid "other" who is not manipulated, terrorized, or
  put off by her problem. You don't have to "walk on eggs"!

It may be liberating for her to learn about your needs. She
can benefit from knowing what feelings her behavior generates
and that a person (you) can report such feelings without in-
dulging in a "see what you made me do" routine. There is an
important difference between acting out anger with yelling or
sullen withdrawal, and being able to say, "I was really upset
about your leaving the office party early to purge."

*Tim went for counseling when he realized his feelings for
Maria were becoming ambivalent: he loved her, but he wanted
to get away from her. The therapist helped him sort out what
he wanted in the relationship and to decide on appropriate
behaviors. Tim would no longer lock the refrigerator, or monitor
her food, or sit quietly when she purged.*

*These limits did not take hold instantly. Maria coyly asked
him to oversee her consumption of peanut butter. Tim refused.
"I'm not your food guard anymore," he told her. When she told*

him she just had to throw up at restaurants, he stopped ac-companying her to restaurants and instead invited her to mov-ies and other nonfood-related activities. As time went on, he no longer wanted to leave her, and she stopped asking him to be her food guard. She began to take more responsibility for herself, and signed up for a workshop on improving body esteem. Tim felt justifiably proud of himself for standing up to her and learning to stop being a codependent.

One way to effectively help without being a codependent is to distinguish between the *person* and the *behavior,* as in the venerable phrase, "Hate the sin, but love the sinner." You may need to repeat many times, "I don't like your food habits, but I care about you." The person with the eating disorder may at first be unable to grasp this distinction. But if you convey that you see her problem and still like her, she can begin to see herself as someone who *has* a problem, rather than someone who *is* a problem.

The best attitude from a spouse is one of caring, coupled with sensible care of oneself, rather than monitoring and guarding the person's food intake or purging. Nobody needs a food or exercise guard, but everyone needs support.

If You Are Entangled or Codependent

If you are entangled or codependent and have not been able to break this pattern on your own, professional advice can be quite useful. These guidelines may also help.

- Eat for yourself, not for her.
- Schedule meals for the convenience of the entire household, without undue concessions to anyone.
- Acknowledge her for who she is and what she does outside the troubled area of food. She has talents, skills, achievements, as well as an eating disorder.
- Be direct about your feelings. When you reach your limit say so. "I don't want to talk about food anymore just now."

- Try to understand how you feel about your body and weight. Then try to separate your own body and food issues from hers. How are they similar? How are they different? If you have trouble with your weight and food, are you taking all the steps you can to help yourself? The answers may help you see yourself more clearly.

Who's in Charge Here?
Two Perspectives on Responsibility

There are two schools of thought about responsibility in human life. One says that all responsibility rests with the individual, who "creates" every success, every disaster, every relationship. This philosophy leaves no room for blame or self-pity, and can stimulate initiative. But a shallow interpretation of it can dignify a "me first" attitude, a selfish indifference to social issues, or a callous dismissal of the person with difficulties.

The other school of thought regards each individual as one cog in the great social machine. The economy, cultural roles, and family values all influence a person. Trying to solve human problems while focusing on too small a perspective is, in this view, as absurd as trying to solve a mystery without going to the scene of the crime. A runaway kid cannot be understood if you do not know what he or she is running away from. Yet, if taken to extremes, this theory can deny individual initiative and permit helplessness or blaming.

In finding a responsible position from which to look at someone struggling with an eating disorder, draw from the wisdom of both schools of thought. The patient is *both* a self-contained human being capable of making choices, and *also* the recipient of larger forces in the world. These forces include a culture obsessed with slimness, riddled with addictions, and plentifully supplied with tempting foods. You are another one of these forces. You did provide certain stimuli, doing and saying things, and she has (consciously or not) decided what to do with them. For instance, you may have encouraged her to be popular in school. She may have decided this was a rule she had to obey.

She may not recognize the available options, and probably does not remember having made certain "decisions." ("I will never trust again." "I don't deserve to be happy.")

One goal of therapy is to help a patient see that her reactions to certain events were not the only options available. Instead of withdrawing, she could have fought back; instead of hating herself, she could have admitted her dislike of someone else.

> *When Kate was young, she withdrew and told herself, I will never eat again; I will never be happy again; I will get sick and then they'll be sorry. She did this in part because she believed the criticisms she heard. She thought her brother, teasing her about her chubbiness, was entitled to tease and that she was obliged to become thin, just the way she had been obligated to take care of the family. Making herself perfect for everyone seemed like the only reasonable choice.*

Most of our patients had choices that they had written out of their world view. Kate, for instance, decided not to actively protest against the influences others had in her life. Instead of complying and developing a symptom, a patient like Kate could have dealt with feeling unpopular, or expressed her needs to her mother. But for each option there was a price she decided (usually out of fear) not to pay. She chose instead the "advantages" of feeling safe and unthreatened. For very good reasons, she was not then able to choose riskier alternatives. Like all of us, she made a trade-off that seemed the best, or only, move at the time. This trade-off was probably influenced by discoveries like these:

- Compliance buys safety from criticism.
- Fat phobia buys relief from other worries.
- Self-hate buys the opportunity to avoid one's own aggressions.
- The go-between role buys a bit of importance.

In therapy, we try to help our patient realize why she made those choices. We help her to see that they made sense at the time, they don't make her a bad person, and that now she can make new choices. We offer coaching, and encourage her to recognize, and act on, her good judgment and preferences. In the same way, you can examine your choices in life and in your interactions with her. *What did I really want? What did I buy with that choice? What do I want now?*

So What Do I Do?

Let's summarize. Even though responsibility for recovery from an eating disorder rests finally with the patient, you can make a positive contribution.

- You can identify the things you do—unwittingly or on purpose — that promote her unhappy feelings. Which ones are you willing to change? Which ones do you feel you need to keep?
- You can support her efforts to change her thinking and behavior.
- You can avoid becoming entangled in her life.

What you can do now is look honestly at your motives. Acknowledge them, see if there is anything in your life that really needs changing, and take care of it. With less pressure from others, the person with an eating disorder has more room to breathe.

> *Joy was relieved when Kate started going to therapy. Maybe now Joy could stop worrying. She had felt guilty that she hadn't been able to solve Kate's problem with her friendship, but now she knew the problem was too complex for that.*
>
> *Soon Joy began to wonder what kind of things happened inside a therapy office. She questioned Kate about this in a friendly, curious way, but Kate would give only very general*

answers. Well, *Joy thought,* things have been better around the apartment lately; I guess I'll just count my blessings.

It felt funny to Joy when Kate developed new habits, such as taking time off one afternoon a week to go to a museum by herself. This made Joy a little jealous—she realized her own life was almost too dependent on planning ahead and getting other people to accompany her. As Kate changed, Joy realized she might have to change too!

CHAPTER 11

Communicating Your Feelings

Despite the best of preparation, you may find yourself tongue-tied when trying to discuss your feelings with the eating disordered person.

- It isn't easy to tell her, "I think you need help."
- It isn't easy to ask her, "Have you been stealing?"
- It isn't easy to say, "I'm sympathetic, but I'm still angry at you."

If there have been long-standing communication blocks in the relationship or the family, beginning anew is doubly difficult—and doubly valuable.[1]

You should also know that many people with eating disorders are poor at communicating. Thinking they should be perfect, they hide true but "unacceptable" feelings. Feeling inferior, they try to project an image of what they "should" be. Thinking other people's needs more important, they neglect to express their own.

Thus, you may not know whether she is sad, or suffering, or angry, because she is more tuned into what *you* may need. Or she may be so numb to her feelings and sensations that she cannot name them. Following are techniques to help you communicate more effectively with your eating disordered friend or relative.

Be prepared to learn things that may challenge you to examine yourself as a person. Your willingness to discuss real feelings may be one of the most important services you can perform.

"I" Language

In American speech, a pattern of blurring the identity of the speaker is very common.

- Instead of saying, "I'm proud of my team's accomplishment," many people say, "You're so excited when your team wins the championship."
- Instead of saying, "I envy you because of that job offer you just turned down," people often say, "You're a fool."
- Instead of saying, "I'm shocked at your behavior," a parent may say, "People of your age are supposed to know better."

This linguistic evasion makes it easy for true messages to get lost amid a flurry of deflection, blame, quoting anonymous authorities, and including hypothetical allies in the discussion. No wonder the eating disordered person communicates poorly— so much miscommunication is all around her!

Using the pronoun "I" means the speaker takes complete responsibility for having that idea or feeling. It lets the hearer know unequivocally who means what. State what you want and believe, feel or know, in sentences that start with "I." This is not a trivial gimmick. Instead of marshalling a hypothetical or even real set of people on your side ("everyone knows" or "we Smiths"), speak for yourself. "I'm the one who loves you and hates to see you suffer." This direct communication is one of the things she is learning to do in her therapy.

Translating Questions

Most questions are not really requests for information, but statements in disguise. Be alert, then, for statements beneath questions.

- The question, "Did you take out the garbage?" may actually be a veiled message of resentment about recent family problems. Rather than asking for information, the speaker may be stating, "I'm angry that you are not doing your share."
- "Can I get you something while I'm at the store?" may mean, "I'm scared you're mad at me for taking the cookies, so I'll do something nice and maybe you won't be mad."
- A college student may ask, "What was college like for you, Dad?" The statement behind the question may be, "I'm frantic that I'm not getting good enough grades. I need to know what yardstick I'll be measured against."
- Behind the question to a friend, "Did you enjoy the movie last night?" may be the statement, "I'm jealous you have time to enjoy yourself."

Learning to detect hidden messages can help you respond accurately to her needs. Sensing the worry behind the question about your college years, you could describe them in a way that admits the uncertainties and strains you too experienced. But do not use this as a sort of interrogation technique. Do not cry, "Aha! I know what you are really saying!"

Secret Dialogue

At times, we all have thoughts we do not wish others to know.

- *Gee, my date looks so pretty; she probably has better opportunities than going out with me.*
- *My boss looks angry today; I wonder if he has discovered I'm below my quota.*
- *This party is boring, but I can't leave yet.*

People with such secret feelings may do very well at hiding them from the outside world. You may recognize this process because no doubt, like everyone, you do it yourself sometimes.

The good news is that, more often than you might expect, your inner feelings can be communicated. Revealing these inner thoughts sometimes leads to relief and closeness. Saying, "I'm really nervous right now" can be a disarming way to break the ice and let the other person know you are human.

It is good to discover this, because difficult messages are exhausting to contain. But they are also difficult to express. A teenage bulimic may be secretly thinking, *I'm afraid that you and Dad aren't getting along.* How can a person lead up to sensitive issues? This leads us to the next topic.

Meta-communication

Meta-communication is a useful skill you may want to learn. This rather long word means "communication about communication itself." It's rather like directing traffic. The speaker steps back from the actual topic of conversation and says things such as this:

- "Wait, I'm getting confused. What did you just say?"
- "Speak louder, I can't hear you."
- "You just interrupted me."
- "Let's take five minutes and cool off."

Such meta-communications help keep the conversation constructive and going in the desired direction.

Meta-communication is especially valuable for difficult conversations. For instance, you notice your parents are bickering and say, "Mom, this is hard for me to say, but I'm afraid that you and Dad aren't getting along." Or it can be helpful when having a fight, telling a secret, or asking a favor you're not sure the other person can fulfill. It's okay to meta-communicate to help say difficult things.

- "This is hard for me to say, but I must confess I'm angry about ..."
- "Please wait a minute while I collect my thoughts."

Choice of Language

The more insecure a person is, the less tolerance he or she will have for judgmental or opinionated language. Words that seem vivid, strong, and even amusing to one person may sting another. How often, indeed, we insult each other with wordplay!

- We call someone "crazy" for bypassing opportunities we desire.
- We exaggerate our reactions in order to be funny.
- We display our puzzlement over another person's tastes.

Our prejudices peep out at every turn. Nothing is wrong with having opinions and preferences, but it stifles the free flow of communication if we judge or ridicule every idea that departs from our own. To the insecure eating disordered person, even the merest hint that someone is judging her opinions can be devastating. It can scare her back into her hiding place.

If you want your eating disordered friend or relative to hear you, try to put the brakes on verbal exuberance. In order not to offend, you may

- Tone down your adjectives. Instead of saying something is "appalling" or "horrible," say it is "unwelcome" or "unpleasant."
- Eliminate red flag words like *obviously* ("Obviously, the man is an idiot") and *should* ("You should know better").
- Acknowledge your preferences and tastes, without assuming they are universal. (To say, "Everyone knows the American cinema is dead" is offensive; "I like Japanese films" isn't.)
- If you must say something negative about someone, use hopeful language. The word *unprepared* leaves room for improvement, while *ignorant* sounds condemning.
- Be specific and use "I" statements if criticism can't be avoided. "I was worried when you left the dinner table early."

The goal here is not to encourage social niceties, but to make honest communications palatable and therefore more likely to be heard.

Asserting and Saying "No"

If the eating disordered person you know is in therapy, she is probably learning to identify her needs and stand up for them. You should be prepared for this new assertiveness. Family and friends sometimes resist changes that occur in a patient during therapy. Who wants to lose the perfect caretaker or the dedicated, straight-A student? You may have to stretch to accommodate her wider range of feelings and wants, but it is for the best. Rejoice: the person you are used to will give way to the healthier person she really is.

The person's new ability to say "no" may confuse you for a while. But it does not require you to surrender all your needs—that would be going to the opposite extreme. The two of you are now in the normal human position of negotiating, day by day, how your two sets of needs and preferences are to be lived out. We only suggest that you give her a little leeway in the beginning, as she tries out new assertiveness skills.

Negotiating

So how do two healthy, communicative persons get along in daily life? They negotiate. Neither one's needs are automatically more important; neither one's tastes are automatically better. Sometimes A will get his or her preference satisfied, sometimes B will. The art is to communicate honestly what each wants, to evaluate facts and feelings, and to leave the door open to further negotiation if new feelings surface.

In many families the idea of negotiation is new: Parents or a dictatorial spouse have ruled by decree. Or signals are so muddled that no clear decision is ever made consciously; things just "end up" one way or another. In a happy family, everyone's needs are considered and important decisions are discussed.

A Checklist for Better Communication

An eating disordered person and her friend or relative may wish to discuss certain matters, but not know how to begin.

We have devised a set of discussion topics, based on our experience in helping people to improve their communications, which can help you get started. Each topic has several options that cover the more common responses you and your partner may have. The reader of this book and the patient may want to sit together, letting this list serve as a guide for discussion. Keep in mind that these are sample questions or requests. Your own topic areas may include other issues, or other responses to these issues.

Some readers may think that this is unnecessary. Isn't this "putting words in people's mouths"? Yet, we have seen over and over that there is a special knack to detecting the *most accurate* message underneath human relations, and that without it communications go astray. We often spend part of therapy sessions helping people uncover things they mean, but can't find words for. These simple phrases condense such therapy sessions and may be of use to you. Feel free to write your ideas on a separate sheet of paper.

The Eating Disordered Person's Requests

About therapy:
- "It's okay to ask about my therapy session."
- "Please don't ask about my therapy session."
- "I'll tell you only a little."
- "It really helps me to share my progress in detail."
- "Come in with me for a session."
- "Please read ... "

About social occasions:
- "Please do not ask me to attend events like buffets or banquets."
- "Ask me and let me decide whether to go."
- "Ask me and help me decide."
- "Ask me once, and if I say no, accept my refusal."

About eating:
- "Please don't feel embarrassed about eating rich desserts in front of me. That only makes me feel guilty."
- "I appreciate it when you forego rich desserts when I am present (as long as it doesn't inconvenience you)."

About the body:
- "It helps when you remind me I really look okay."
- "I can't really believe praise yet, but I'm trying!"
- "Please don't talk about my body. I worry about it too much."
- "Please try to concentrate on my other attributes."

About feelings:
- "Please comfort me when I'm upset. The signals are _____ _____ ."
- "Please don't intrude when I'm upset. I'm learning to handle things myself, and I need practice."
- "Listen to my anger. It's part of life."
- "Please don't try to make me stop being sad, excited, grouchy, or whatever."
- "Please do not try to use logic when I'm having feelings."
- "It helps me if you tell me I'm going too far."
- "It helps me if you tell me some of your feelings."

When someone says worriedly, "But I thought you were getting better. ..."
- "I am! The anesthetic is wearing off."
- "I've had a setback, but I'm confident I'll move forward."
- "I've had ups and downs and my therapist is helping me."
- "You don't need to worry about my therapy—it's personal."
- "I'm glad you asked. I'm a bit discouraged. Let's talk."

Other requests from the eating disordered person:
- "I really appreciate it when you ..."
- "It really bothers me when you ..."

The Partner's Requests

About your disorder:
- "I've read a lot and understand what you're going through."
- "This is all new to me."
- "I just don't get it; it's hard to relate to this problem."
- "I'm scared about the medical risks."

About therapy:
- "Give me time to get used to the idea of therapy."
- "Let me tell you my experiences in therapy."
- "I don't want to hear too many details."
- "I'll try to restrain my curiosity!"

About the partner's needs:
- "I'm wrestling with guilt. Let me know if I hover too much."
- "I resent the financial burden."
- "I wish you'd accept and believe my admiration and love."

After eight months of therapy, Kate felt ready to deal with her brother. She hadn't forgotten that dreadful night when she had learned about his accident, and how she had binged and made herself sick with worry. "But what do I say to him?" she asked Andrea. "I can't say, 'You're a bum for drinking and driving.' "

"Listen to what you just said," Andrea replied. "You assumed you had to either say nothing, or call him a bum. There are other ways to communicate about such things!" Andrea then showed Kate how many other possible things she could say. She could say, "I was terribly frightened for you." She could say, "Scott, I don't approve of your drinking, and I hope you rethink your habits because you mean so much to me." Or she could say, "I was angry!"

Kate needed a lot of practice before she could feel comfortable even thinking about such messages. "He's still on crutches," she said. "Wouldn't it be mean to lay my stuff on him now?"

Andrea pointed out Kate's temptation to squash her feelings in order to protect her brother. "People can stand the truth, you know," Andrea told Kate. "Sometimes it's even a relief!"

After a few sessions, Kate was ready to visit Scott. To her surprise, it was easier than she expected to come out from behind her facade and be real with him. Strangely enough, it even made them closer! He began telling her more about his life than he had in years.

Developing Your Own Checklist

You and the eating disordered person may want to develop your own checklist (written or unwritten) to supplement what we have offered above. Here are guidelines for creating your own list:

Choosing Topics to Discuss

What areas of your life embarrass you or do you try to avoid? Medical problems, money, social occasions, sex? These are the very ones that may need to be discussed.

How to Create the Request

Each person should take a moment to think about the topic (for instance, money), noting any feelings of resentment or puzzlement the topic brings. Resentment is not a crime, it's a clue! It's a way to discover what you want, since resentment is a sign you aren't getting it. So use it as a signal to lead you to the thing you do want. When both parties have figured out what they want, write it down.

How to Approach the Task

Think of this as a *shared task,* not a fearful reminder of danger, or as an opportunity to criticize. If feelings of fear or anger are rather strong, it may be preferable to develop your checklist with the help of a third party. Or you can put off this task until the feelings have been worked through and the way is clear for skill-building. Remember to use *meta-communication* as you work together. Either person can say, "I'm tired, let's stop for a while," or "I'm a bit nervous about the next item." Any request can be thought of as an experimental guideline, to be tested, refined, or replaced as needed. This is not a test of your ability to solve everything today!

A final observation: Sometimes friends and family feel frustrated because the eating disordered person doesn't seem to accept their love and respect. She turns aside praise, or says, "You can't mean that," and goes on being unhappy. Why? Partly it's because she knows her faults and may dwell on them too much. Secretly, she may be thinking, *If they* really *knew me, they wouldn't say they like me.* Not liking herself, she can't believe anyone else would. So anyone offering praise must be insincere or crazy.

You might say quietly, "I didn't say that for you—I said it for me. I *wanted* to say 'I love you.' " Or you could lighten the tone and say, "Yeah! I'm crazy—I like you, even with your faults!"

CHAPTER 12

Living with the Eating Disordered Person

Living with a person who has an eating disorder can be complicated. Setting limits, knowing what to say, and managing communal supplies are all part of the picture. In this chapter we will look at three further aspects: the body image, holidays, and indecisiveness.

What to Say about the Body

Many anorexics and bulimics have distorted images of their body size. They feel fat and ugly even when all the evidence points to the contrary. A person who doubts her attractiveness—and that goes for most adolescents—may remember for years a disparaging comment made by a friend or relative. One young woman recalled bitterly, "I'll never forget what my grandfather said the night of the prom. I had spent weeks getting ready. And he grumbled to my mother, 'Well, I guess that's the best you could do with a blimp.' "

In some families, "correct" size and appearance are habitual topics of conversation. The sons are encouraged to eat and become big football players, while the daughters are monitored for food and weight so they will look like cheerleaders. If the inherited body type doesn't fit these demands, the young person may feel like a failure. In other cases, what lingers in the child's mind is just an offhand remark, made by a relative who is not really an insensitive person—but the hearer felt belittled and never forgot. Many adults, for instance, can't seem to forget hearing, as a child, comments such as, "You're not as pretty as your sister."

Today (perhaps hoping to compensate for past comments, or because you are genuinely mystified by her dislike of her body) you may have the urge to insist to the food-preoccupied family member that she looks fine. Sometimes family members hope to bring an anorexic or bulimic to her senses by showering her with compliments about her appearance. But a person with an eating disorder does not see herself or hear others with any degree of clarity. Such repetitious attempts to persuade may only make her feel misunderstood. ("Can't they SEE how fat I am? Don't they know how important it is to look perfect?") What can you do?

You can try to counter the harmful effects of television and magazine advertising by affirming a person's beautiful qualities, spiritual as well as physical. Praising a person's clean hair, glowing expression, good posture, and inner quality of assurance and warmth can help youngsters learn that beauty is more than fashion—or fashionable thinness.

If an eating disorder is already in place, you may not be able to do much directly to overcome her glum certainty that she is unattractive. You can, however, offer help by omission. After stating your opinion that she looks fine, let the subject go— don't get hooked into a lengthy discussion evaluating her body. You can praise some feature you really like, and stand by your opinion until she finds that her self-deprecating remarks will not draw you into a fruitless discussion of her flaws.

Holidays and Special Events

Jennifer has come home for the Christmas holidays. She looks preoccupied. Her hours are unusual: she sleeps until noon, and her parents can hear her moving around in the kitchen until 3:00 A.M. At Thanksgiving they had noticed something a bit strange about her eating. She would load up her plate at meals, then ignore the food for most of the meal. Then, she would eat a lot of food rapidly and push away her plate with an exclamation of self-criticism. Christmas is coming, and with the family arriving, special treats and events have been prepared. Jennifer's brother and sister are here. Is there anything to worry about? her mother wonders. How should I treat her?

Holidays and occasions like weddings, reunions, and graduations bring extra pressure on the eating disordered person. Special occasions not only inspire people to prepare rich food, but also focus attention on personal appearance. Everywhere reminders show us how we are "supposed" to be: thin and happy, carefree, eating lightly, sharing good news. You can help your eating disordered person if you keep the following guidelines in mind:

- Be prepared for awkward moments. This doesn't mean you must start conversations about how terrible things will be. A simple remark, made once, can relieve pressure she may be feeling: "I know the holiday season may be stressful for you. Let me know how I can help." Then be available to talk over feelings and problem situations, so she doesn't feel isolated.
- Don't offer her sugary treats.
- Include nonfood events in gatherings, such as playing games, singing, or taking walks.
- Experiment with low-calorie foods, without making her food needs the center of everyone's attention. Include low-calorie options in your party menus, as well as the conventional party food. Then she has a choice. Other guests may also appreciate food with less saturated fat and cholesterol.
- Don't force her to go to events she doesn't wish to attend.
- Don't deter her from eating before a major event. She may be doing so to be able to avoid the buffet table. This may be an

important intermediate step for her in steering clear of the most stressful situations.
- If she asks for help in setting limits, help. If she doesn't ask, don't. Even if you enter an agreement with her, be prepared for her to change her mind.

When a friend or relative is coming home for the holidays after being away for some months, friends and relatives may be worried about her appearance and start hovering, advising, worrying, and attempting to cure her on the spot. This is understandable, but probably counterproductive. Find other things to talk about. Current events, movies, the arts, books you've read, family news—all are good subjects for conversation. If you are worried, express concern about her as a whole person, not just about her diet and figure.

Normal household rules should be followed. Don't let your concern and sympathy mislead you into thinking that rule-bending would help. All adult members of a household, including one with an eating disorder, need to act like responsible adults. If she asks you to empty the house of binge foods, decide what you can realistically eliminate, and be frank with her about it.

At the same time, there is no reason to deny the whole family any traditional treats. You need neither hide them nor offer them more than once. But avoid demanding that she express her appreciation for your cooking artistry by consuming enormous portions.

After reading these recommendations, sit back and let them sink in for a moment. Imagine yourself following the guidelines that apply in your situation—and then relax. This is not a test. Holidays are meant to be a respite from the everyday, not the time to enforce strict rules or embark on an intensive appraisal of the problem. Holidays are to be enjoyed.

Indecisiveness

The person with an eating disorder may have difficulty making decisions. This shows most visibly with respect to food.

Should she stick to the diet, or give in and eat? Now that she has had two cookies, should she go ahead and have six?

But indecision also shows up in other areas of life. Major turning points such as choosing a college, or selecting among careers, can trigger a flurry of panic. You may see her nervously reviewing her options, seeking other people's opinions, and becoming excessively anxious. Retreating to food can occur at these times. Or you may not see the indecision: she agonizes in private.

Why are decisions so difficult for eating disordered people? Remember, we're talking about a *perfectionist* here—a person who assumes there is a perfect decision, that life consists of "right" options that successful people discover without trial and error. Living properly consists of making the "right" choice the first time, so she had better detect which one it is! In this world view, there is no tolerance for error or ambiguity.

Whether the options are relatively different from each other (a huge state university versus a small liberal arts college), or relatively similar (two small liberal arts colleges), anguishing takes place. She can imagine in excruciating detail the consequences of the decision, and perhaps is playing them out in her mind—with mostly negative features, you can be sure! Convinced that others are judging, she judges herself.

- *I should have already decided.*
- *If I were really on the ball, I would have better options.*
- *I can't do that job, and everyone will find out.*

She may believe she can, and should, *have it all*, a kind of expectation of omnipotence. A person who believes this does not know that to get one thing, you generally have to relinquish other things. The myth of "superwoman," though well debunked in some quarters, might still be influencing her.

There may also be *ambivalence* (conflicting feelings). She may want one option, but have reservations about it. (Don't we all!) She may long for a promotion, but fear the responsibility. She may like one potential dating partner, but feel safer with another. She may want to stop taking care of the world, but still feel responsibility for others.

To top it off, she *dreads regrets*. Knowing herself all too well, she knows that whatever she decides, she will beat up on herself for it tomorrow. Who wouldn't agonize over a decision if he or she knew that criticism would be the inevitable result? Eating is often a way of delaying decisions, or soothing the accompanying anxiety.

What can you do?

- Remind your loved one that mistakes are a part of life. (Maybe even share some of your own howlers, especially ones that turned out well in the end.)
- Restrict criticism of her decisions unless asked, or unless it is absolutely necessary.
- Model good decision-making.
- Listen sympathetically, but do not let yourself be drawn into unproductive agonizing.

CHAPTER 13

Special Groups: Children

Children may begin worrying about their bodies and actively attempting to diet as early as age nine or ten, causing their parents and health care professionals great concern. Even younger children may have eating problems. While not full-blown eating disorders, these are important to notice and correct before they get out of hand.

Sometimes a child's eating problems may reflect a larger family problem such as conflict between the parents or other family stress. Other times, parents are unsure how best to feed a child and may feed inappropriately. They may not know how to interpret the baby's or child's hunger and fullness signals, and may unknowingly push food on a full baby, or not feed a hungry one. Sometimes, the more a baby or child refuses food, the harder the parents push. This sets up a vicious cycle: the child feels her basic hunger and fullness signals are misunderstood, and the parents are frustrated by this seemingly impossible child.

For example, finicky eating may be the focus of so much attention that the child can become self-conscious about eating. According to noted family therapist and nutritionist, Ellyn Satter, a parent's job is to prepare and offer three healthy meals a day and appropriate snacks.[1] The child's job is to eat. Children should not be prodded to overeat or undereat; this can feel like an invasion, making mealtimes a battleground. Satter also suggests postponing heated arguments or debates to other times so that mealtimes remain safe for enjoyable conversation.

Let's look at the unfolding of a child's relationship to food. Each stage of child development brings joys and problems. This is true in play, language, and motor skills, as well as in food and eating.

The Infant

An infant needs physical and emotional comfort. She needs to feel cared about and responded to. If she is fed when hungry and changed when wet, the infant knows she is "heard." Learning what a baby wants and when she wants it is a challenge for any parent. These signals may not be easy to decipher, and parents may give food when the baby wants to cuddle, or offer a toy when she is hungry.

When the baby turns away from the bottle or breast and seems full, this is a signal. The alert parent will know this means "no more food" and stops offering it. This means the parent trusts the infant to know her hunger, and the infant is then reinforced in her self-knowledge. When such signals are accurately read, a foundation of good communication is laid that promotes trust and enhances the child's development. Of course, no parent is perfect. Learning to live with error is a necessary life skill for both parent and infant.

The Toddler

The toddler, like the infant, is busy exploring and learning. She is more mobile, and is learning to talk. Saying "no" to the parent and the world gives her a thrilling sense of power. Saying "yes" and "no" to parental expectations about food is an inevitable part of this "toddler power" exercise. *Will they force me to eat?* she wonders. *Will they let me throw food at my brother? What if I spill by accident? What if I spill on purpose? How many cookies can I have?* Tempting though it may be to demand cleanliness and good table manners, remember that at this early stage, each meal is a scene in the child's drama of growth and experimentation. It is important for the child to know that you sense this.

Children at this age can be taught to recognize feelings. They can be asked, "Are you feeling tired, sad, happy, thirsty, hungry?" As they learn to pick out their feelings from this list, they also come to recognize the wide range of emotions they have and to identify sensations of hunger from feelings such as anger or loneliness.

The match between the child's abilities and the parent's expectations is important. Each parent must decide when to just let the child be, and when to set limits. Parents can regularly question themselves to set appropriate limits.

> *When Joe had picked up two-year-old Aaron's plate of spilled food from the floor for the fifth time and Aaron began shrieking at the top of his lungs, Joe thought he was going to lose his wits. He asked himself,* Is this too much for me? Yes. Then I need to get Aaron to his room if he won't stop crying at the table. Otherwise I'll blow up. He and I both need a time out.

> *Sandra really wanted to get lunch over with so that she could take daughter, Ceci, to the store. She had errands she just had to do. Then she noticed that Ceci was elbow-deep in mashed potatoes. She thought,* Since all three year olds put their fingers in the mashed potatoes, I won't fuss about it, but will nicely remind Ceci that I'd like to see her use her fork rather than her fingers to eat mashed potatoes. Then I can sponge her arms off and leave.

If parents got paid for the energy and inner dialogue we expend to parent well, we'd all be millionaires!

Firm rules are crucial with very small children. Parents should train children to expect certain foods at certain times. The three-year-old who announces to his mother that he wants nothing but cookies for lunch—and gets them—is headed for trouble.

He does not understand nutrition and won't for many years; he does, however, understand "no," and caring parents will say it.

The Four- to Six-Year-Old

When can a child be expected to show responsibility for neatness and decorum? Increased expectations must be matched to the child's age and personality. Some parents expect a four-year-old to be as mannerly as a nine-year-old. Unable to meet their expectations, the four-year-old child will fail — dismaying himself and them. If, on the other hand, parents treat their four-year-old as though he were still two, he will probably accept the permission and act less responsibly than he could. A very dextrous child with good concentration may be able to learn manners more easily than a child who is less coordinated or one who has trouble being still and concentrating.

A parent's job is to encourage the child to grow and mature, and to make the child's necessary challenges small enough to be manageable. A toddler will pick up his spoon when ready. A five-year-old can tell you his favorite kind of pizza and where to get it. Such milestones can be great fun for both parent and child. The real test is keeping one's patience until the child is ready. The bright, new behavior sometimes fades when the child is tired or under stress. Parents should understand and forgive "slips" back to old, babyish behaviors.

The sheer quantity of lessons about food and life that must be taught to a small child can feel burdensome. Remember that the child has many years to learn these lessons, and they will be taught many times over—at least three times a day. You will have many chances to correct mistakes.

Julie is four. Now that she uses a fork and spoon at the table with some skill, her parents expect her to eat what is put in front of her. They applaud every bite she takes, instruct her to chew it well, and comment on her table manners. Their conversation with each other takes a backseat to the topic of Julie's eating. Suddenly Julie stops eating, meal after meal. Her mother and father cajole, threaten, and plead at every meal, but Julie is resolute.

Now Julie, who has quit eating to express resentment at her parents' intrusive control of her eating, has discovered a wonderful way to get attention. It is more exciting than food.

Taking a counselor's advice, the parents begin to leave Julie in peace at the table. It takes great self-control, but they let her play with the food on her plate and do not insist on her eating it. They chat with her and with each other about other topics, while Julie gradually absorbs the idea that this particular game is over. She can go back to eating again.

Four- to six-year-olds need to be allowed to develop their own unique food and eating styles within parental limits. They need to continue to develop a relationship with food and, at the same time, become ready to begin to learn adult manners.

The School-Aged Child

When children leave the familiar home or preschool environment and go to school, they see the world around them from a new vantage point. They begin to acquire more cultural perceptions about fat and thin, healthy and unhealthy. They learn our society's prejudice against large-sized people and they begin to evaluate their bodies critically. They may even tease fat people or be teased about their own bodies.

Parents' attitudes about their bodies influence the sensitive six- to-ten-year-old.

- *Does Mom like her body?*
- *What does she say about getting older with her body?*
- *If she doesn't like hers, how can I like mine?*

These are years of intense body-esteem development and parents should be aware of a child's extreme vulnerability to comments about her body. She will not always forget unkind words, especially if they become part of the family "humor." Parents who don't like their bodies should try to improve this painful relationship to themselves and at the same time give their child the message that her body is a good one, whatever its size and shape. This is very important. Children often come to parents complaining about their bodies' insufficiencies and they need reassurance that they are okay.

Appreciating your daughter's change toward womanhood is also crucial. Her added fat and curves are the normal first steps to becoming a grown-up lady. If parents provide this kind of support and work with building body-esteem, exercise and fitness become ways to have a good time, rather than ways to make a "bad" body "good."

Girls often begin *playing* at dieting at a preteen stage or even earlier. This is not unusual. But if they begin *dieting in earnest*, this is not something to laugh off. Parents should emphasize healthy, low-fat eating for the family, and exercise that is fun, but the dangers of dieting should be made clear. Encouraging a child to diet is usually a mistake. Children should be allowed to reach their full growth before restricting food for weight loss. They also need the support of parents who won't join our society's dieting madness.

As anyone who has dieted knows, it is very hard work. Most adult dieters fail to maintain their desired weights—if they ever reach them! Children will model parental behavior. If dieting seems desirable to the parents, children will try to follow suit. Developing a healthful family food and exercise style is a more productive approach than going on the diet merry-go-round with your child.

With proper training, children at this stage can understand the roles of protein, fats, and carbohydrates in the diet and can identify the basic food groups. They can also be taught the importance of body fat. Fat insulates us from excessive heat and cold, helps us feel comfortable while sitting, cushions internal organs, and provides stored energy. Knowledge helps us to build body-esteem and create respect for food, eating, and the body.

Teenagers

When puberty begins, usually at age ten to thirteen (although for some children it begins as early as eight), the child's earlier beliefs and attitudes may be severely tested. Teenagers become self-conscious about their bodies as hormones work their natural transformations. The teenager will just as naturally start rebelling, questioning, and testing her own limits. Do Mom's and Dad's ideas about food, alcohol, and life make sense? What if the peer group is drinking, or bingeing and throwing up?

Good communication is essential. Parents often find it hard to allow teenagers to learn their own strengths and to make mistakes and fail. It helps if the parents have thought through the problems and decided how far they should allow their children to go. Parents should separate enough from their growing child to let her experiment to learn the consequences of her behavior. But at the same time, parents should set limits that stop the teen from seriously harming herself. A limit may not be perfectly placed, but it will give some security to both parents and children.

Parents at this stage often blame themselves for "messing up" their kids. The kids are eager to agree; they now know their parents are less than perfect, and they may have become experts at pushing the parental guilt button. But accepting an adolescent's critical attitude defeats the task of the teenager's learning to accept responsibility for his or her life. It also interferes with getting teens the help they need. You can admit you are not perfect, and have weaknesses, and still assume a strong parental role.

Teenagers, and especially teenage boys, can have very large appetites. All that growing and maturing (not to mention sports and dancing) consume calories. Girls' caloric needs increase only slightly in this period. Active kids with large appetites need to be encouraged to see their large caloric needs as normal rather than "gross." Kids who watch a lot of television, however, may not be meeting their needs for strenuous physical activity.

Kids who eat some meals at home every day that include fruits, vegetables, whole grains, and lean proteins and milk, are being provided with the basics. Then, the occasional extra hamburgers, fries, and shakes are no cause for alarm.

Rule-setting Is an Important Task for Any Parent

In the teenage years, limits are often severely tested. An adolescent is expanding her horizons and responsibilities, yet may also long for the safe containment of childhood, when her excesses were restrained by parental firmness.

> *Looking good had always been important to Kristie. Now in her senior year in high school, she dressed beautifully, had a boyfriend, took aerobics classes, was an honor student, and never stopped going. She demanded a 1:00 A.M. weekday curfew and a 3:00 A.M. curfew on weekends. Her mother, Laura, busy with two younger children and impressed by Kristie's maturity, gave in. Kristie demanded an allowance for clothes and classes that was really more than the budget could stand, but again Laura gave in. Now Laura was worried about the way Kristie kept losing weight.*
>
> *Laura felt guilty because she had been busy working and attending school when Kristie was small. But it seemed that the more she gave in, the more demands Kristie made. When Kristie ate and purged an entire chocolate cake Laura had made for friends, and then casually confessed that she "couldn't help it," Laura finally became angry. She shouted at Kristie and a moment later said, "That's it. I need someone to talk to."*
>
> *The therapist Laura chose helped her set rules, and encouraged her to get support from friends, family, and even Kristie's school counselor. She helped Laura stand her ground when*

Kristie tested the limits. As soon as Kristie found her mother
did not back down, she began to obey the family rules.

Laura also explored other areas of life that bothered her. The
daughter of an alcoholic mother, she had always wanted a
household without anger and "fuss." In trying to create peace,
however, she had failed to be firm. Laura joined an Al-Anon-
sponsored Adult Children of Alcoholics group and found this
very beneficial in understanding herself and in helping Kristie.

Adolescence is the time full-blown eating disorders tend to
emerge. No longer a child, the adolescent is trying to put all
the pieces together to go out and face the world. She wants to
fit in, to be adult. She wants to be herself, but is not always
certain what that self is. It is a time of great hormonal change
as her body surges toward womanhood, and of great psychological change as well. Her brain matures still more, and her
ability to think abstractly and reason increases.

Many adolescents flirt with some mild form of bingeing,
compulsive eating, or dieting. This does not mean they are
eating disordered. Some teenagers can pass through a mild,
try-it-on-for-size phase of unhealthful eating, but it doesn't really
fit and they give it up on their own. Others get stuck and
cannot find a way out.

For example, if a girl has been overcontrolled and held to
impossibly high standards, she has, by adolescence, internal-
ized such messages and will be acting on them—perhaps by
overcontrolling her appetite, perhaps by going all the way and
bingeing. If she has felt neglected and her childhood has been
marked by family conflict and chaos, she may resort to food for
solace and then try to escape the consequences by purging.

Parents or others important in her life can show they care
and are optimistic, rather than to fix blame or fall into hopeless
resignation. Get her into treatment. Learn to listen: she will
have less need of sending a distress signal like anorexia or
compulsive eating if she knows that her feelings are heard and
understood. Also, take inventory of your needs and limits so

you don't find yourself constantly "walking on eggs." Examine your goals and dreams, and make sure you aren't planning for her to fulfill them for you. Let her surprise you. (She will, in any event.)

In dealing with food-conscious teens, it's a good idea to let them participate in meal planning and in other household decisions. But let their emancipation be gradual, and welcomed by you, rather than resisted. The goal is not perfection but learning.

If weight management is a genuine problem for your teenager, you might consider recommending a program like Laurel Mellin's SHAPEDOWN, offered by many hospitals and clinics nationwide. SHAPEDOWN takes a group of teenagers through a program manual that covers body-esteem, food management, exercise, and other key elements of a healthy lifestyle; it is about how to be healthy rather than how not to be fat.[2]

CHAPTER 14

Special Groups: Men and Boys

Though most people with eating disorders are women, some experts estimate men and boys account for up to 10 percent of eating disorder patients. Like women, men can be bulimics, anorexics, compulsive eaters, or have a combination of these conditions. And like women, they suffer with their problems.

Jeffrey knew he was overweight: he had been since child-hood. By age forty he felt he had tried every diet ever devised, and then some. But he just couldn't seem to keep weight off. At Jeffrey's annual checkup, his doctor mentioned that Jeffrey really ought to lose twenty-five pounds. He referred Jeffrey to a nutritionist. Here we go again, thought Jeffrey. But this time he decided to be honest. To his surprise, he found himself telling the nutritionist that he had been eating compulsively since childhood and had begun purging earlier in the year. He described how he hid food in his desk at work, and sneaked down to the candy machines when he thought no one was looking. After overcoming his embarrassment, he was relieved to have finally told someone.

There seem to be varying meanings to eating disorders in men, depending on the age. Researchers find that eating disorders in boys under age thirteen tend to reflect family problems. From ten to twenty-five, young men's problems with food resemble those of young women: they are intensely absorbed with body image and trying to look good. Young men, however, tend to be more interested in defining muscle and avoiding flab than young women. The reported incidence of eating disorders in men twenty-six and older diminishes rapidly, probably reflecting the fact that men either don't come in for treatment or else their eating disorder is overlooked by well-intentioned but uninformed health professionals.[1] There is no reason to believe that men stop worrying about their weight at the magic age of twenty-six!

The Challenge Men Face in Middle Age

Like women, many men struggle all their lives with a genetic predisposition toward obesity. In their thirties, forties, and fifties, the struggle intensifies as metabolism slows and lifestyle changes: the athlete becomes the gardener, the all-night dancer becomes the couch potato. Add a physician's stern warnings about high blood pressure and heart disease, and panic can set in. The result might be a sensible program of exercise and nutrition—or it might be a siege of compulsive eating and even purging.

Fortunately, in general, men appear to be more realistic about their ideal weight than women are. Men are less likely to use diet pills, but more likely to have histories of substance abuse. These research findings come from a study that also places homosexual and bisexual men at higher risk for eating disorders than heterosexual men, possibly because of a subcultural preference for leanness.[2] Other studies show a higher incidence of eating disorders among men in professions which demand thinness, such as entertainment or sports which require staying in a certain weight category (such as jockeys and wrestlers).[3]

Why do men develop eating disorders? For some of the same reasons women do—to avoid ridicule, or to gain acceptance and love. We have heard many stories about the merciless teasing and humiliation that fat children are subjected to. The average male with an eating disorder, according to another study, is about 21 percent overweight before dieting—much more obese than his female counterpart.[4] They were determined to diet away the taunts of cruel schoolmates and family members.

> *Fred is twenty-four. He's tall, dark and handsome, and defi-nitely on the fast track, having been hired directly out of school by a top law firm. He began bingeing and purging in college. The habit really became entrenched when he studied for the bar exam. Now with the stress of a new job, and his expectation to make a big splash at work, he throws up lunch even if he eats a normal amount. When his cousin told him about O.A., Fred agreed to accompany her to a meeting, and listened with all his might. What he heard made him realize that he was living with self-hate, just as these people were. His achieve-ments and perfectionism were just like what they talked about! His eating and purging habit was a distraction from worries. He attended more meetings, and saw that his demands on himself were just a way of trying to measure up, to be acceptable.*
>
> *To Fred's surprise, he became fascinated by the inner world. Who would ever have guessed that this logical, hard-driving guy would choose to spend three evenings a week talking about feelings with a bunch of strangers? But as he realized the image he presented to the world wasn't his true self, he began to experiment with other things—yoga, swimming, music. His girlfriend was delighted when more time seemed to open up in Fred's life to be with people. She saw that he was not always stoic, that sometimes he needed to lean as well as be leaned on. Their relationship deepened. His bingeing and purg-ing tapered off, then stopped. He found, like many ex-purgers, that his weight did not go up and that he felt better now.*

How Men Face up to Impossible Ideals

Twenty years ago, a man's physique seemed to have less bearing on his social acceptability than did his manners, intel-ligence, character, and ability to make money. Now the same advertising machine that has always held impossible ideals for women is doing the same for men, who acutely feel a pressure to look lean and fit into the latest fashions. It is not enough to be the debonair, successful man—one must also be the Nautilus Man with well-defined muscles and trim abdomen. One shaving-cream ad boasted, "With just one lathering, this man will like mirrors better."

Double messages about manhood abound. The "real man" takes seconds, even if his doctor wants him to take smaller firsts. A real man eats desserts and drinks all the alcohol he wants. A real man isn't afraid of meat, steak, *man* food. Some products even contain the name "man" in their labels, with large portions of fat-rich foods. The messages for men are becoming as contradictory as those for women: Be thin but eat like a he-man. Never show emotion, but play with children. Work long hours and make lots of money, but look rested and find time to be a master racquetball player.

This cultural pressure begins early. Boys, like girls, are encouraged to believe there is only one "right" kind of body. This is evident in children's toys. Dolls are unrealistically thin, and even the muscle-bound war heroes and space creatures have tiny waists. Obviously, this is an unhealthy influence for boys as well as for girls.

Thus, appearance-madness is affecting men too. We already see a kind of weight-consciousness in high school and college age men that was unheard of in their parents' generation. It may well be that the immunity from criticism that males once enjoyed is going the way of the dinosaur. If that is so, doctors' offices will see increasing numbers of young men trying to look like pop music star Michael Jackson or body builder-turned-actor Arnold Schwarzenegger.

With a shorter history of body image obsession, men also have less tradition in fighting fat. They are less familiar with the panoply of diet books, low calorie food products, and other diet paraphernalia. Given the role of dieting in creating fat and eating disorders, perhaps this is a good thing!

Though more unusual, an eating disorder in a male does not mean that he is necessarily more ill than a female with a similar problem. There is no reason to treat a male bulimic or anorexic patient with more worry than a female. There may be some impediments to treatment: fewer health professionals are aware of men's eating problems and men may be reluctant to seek treatment; also, fewer psychotherapists understand the nuances of eating disorders in men. Some men who call us to inquire about treatment do not leave a return phone number or cannot bring themselves to make an appointment. Others begin treatment and are helped. We hope that society and the health professions will learn to understand and help men with eating problems.

CHAPTER 15

There May be Other Problems

Eating disorders may be part of a larger picture of confusion and suffering. In this chapter we'll look at other problems patients may wrestle with: impulsivity and stealing, drug and alcohol use, and suicidal feelings.

Impulsivity and Stealing

Impulsivity means a tendency to give in to sudden whims, rather than to evaluate or resist them. An impulsive person may punch someone, accept a ride with a stranger, buy expensive items irresponsibly, or in other ways fail to use good judgment. Sometimes such impulsive acts create serious harm.

Among people with eating disorders, the kinds of impulsive behaviors we worry about most—apart from uncontrolled eating, of course—are stealing and substance use. Impulsivity seems to appear more with bulimics.[1] Bulimics may steal their binge food or other items such as laxatives. They may be

- eating themselves out of house and home and not be able to pay for their habit without stealing;
- stealing other things as a kind of consolation;
- enjoying the contrast from their usual "good girl" facade;
- getting a thrill from expressing resentment and getting away with it; or
- making a call for help, hoping to be caught and stopped.

There are consequences: the person who steals tends to hide the illegal action, and become even more secretive and ashamed in her relationships with other people. Family and housemates may be torn between wanting to protect their own legitimate interests, and not wanting to confront a person who is already fragile. If caught, she now may have legal problems in addition to everything else.

> *Kate came late to her session one day. She avoided looking at Andrea, and her conversation was scattered and stilted. Finally, with a look of misery on her face, she blurted out her embarrassing secret. On impulse, she had stolen a garment the day before from a local store, stuffing it under her skirt and walking out without paying. Now she was terrified, sure she would be caught. But even worse, she was afraid she would do it again. "Does that mean I'm a criminal now?" she asked. She wondered how she could undo her action without getting caught.*

Whatever the reason a person steals, it is wrong. But a confrontation needs to be handled delicately: you should not be so forceful as to frighten her into silence or to forfeit your leverage as a concerned family member or friend. Start by tackling one situation at a time. "Mary, I can't find the ice cream I was saving for my friends' visit tonight. Did you take it?"

She may deny taking it. It is awfully embarrassing to admit our shortcomings, especially if we have engaged in something as antisocial as stealing. Denial is common. In this case you have two options: decline to push the matter further, or confront her. If you feel strongly about the situation, then it is likely that you will want to do the latter.

This can be an exercise in diplomacy, but worth it in the end. Allowing property lines to be confused only perpetuates the problem. The three C's—Clarity, Calm (talking forcefully but not yelling), and Communication — are needed.

It helps, when confronting, to have convincing evidence. "Mary, it was there an hour ago, and no one else has been here." She may continue to deny. It is important that you tell her how you see things. Be assertive without resorting to screaming. For example, "Mary, I really do think you ate the ice cream and I feel bad about that because I needed it for my guests. I realize you have a problem, but that doesn't give you the right to take things. If you wanted ice cream you could have bought your own. Please don't let this happen again."

The same holds true if you suspect a friend or roommate is stealing from stores, the consequences of which can certainly be more serious. We have also seen a number of people with eating disorders who work in food service jobs and steal food. A person caught stealing faces consequences in terms of job, relationships, self-esteem, and the law.

Kids and Stealing

If you are the parent of a minor child or adolescent who has been stealing, it is time to set firm rules and perhaps to consult your pediatrician, therapist, or parenting self-help group for guidance. This can be especially important if limit-setting has been difficult for you in the past. There are many ways to set and uphold limits in loving and effective ways.

At seven, Benjamin was not bulimic or anorexic. But he surely liked to eat and take food from the kitchen and hoard it in his room. He also liked to leave the grocery store with little bits of food in his hand or in his pocket. Justine, his mother, was at her wits' end. What with his whining for sweets and continually walking out of the grocery store with candies and other items, she felt ready to scream. He wasn't fat; he just seemed to love food—too much. Justine's pediatrician suggested she see a child psychologist for advice.

The psychologist helped Justine learn to set limits on talking about food and on stealing. Rules were set, and it was explained to Benjamin that he could earn "points" by following the rules or lose "points" by breaking them:

1. *He could talk about food no more than twice an hour. Any more, and he lost two points.*
2. *Stealing food (or anything else) meant losing ten points.*
3. *He could earn points for doing homework and household chores.*
4. *He could cash in his points, not for material things but for special time with Mom or Dad.*

Benjamin was told, in a kind and patient manner, that his parents valued contact and communication. In fact, they valued them so much that they were going to go to a special teacher (therapist) who would help them have better contact and communication between themselves and with him. They were now able to see that their intense fighting over the past year and Benjamin's food preoccupation and stealing were related.

In this case, the child's behavior reflected the family situation. The parents' fighting, which had gotten so much worse lately, had triggered their son's whining and hoarding behavior. It was as if Benjamin was stocking up "love" against a vaguely sensed terrifying parental break-up. Once his parents began facing and resolving differences, he stopped hoarding and whining and began to take more of an interest in his toys and games.

With an older child, issues tend to be more complex. Sometimes an adolescent's behavior is so out of control—with flagrant abuse of authority, stealing and other crimes, substance abuse, promiscuity, or more serious mental health problems—that enrollment in a residential treatment center is the best choice. This is a full-time program in which the youngster is placed away from home to work with a team of counselors and other professionals. Therapists, courts, physicians, and parents often make the decision together to enroll the youngster in a hospital or other residential program. Peer support programs based on the "tough love" ideas have also helped many parents who believed their situations were beyond help. Tough love involves giving children very strict and clear limits, and backing that up with a cohesive local network of other tough love parents.

Alcohol and Other Drug Abuse

Substances of many kinds are used and misused in our society. From the ancient substance of wine to the most modern "designer drugs," liquids, powders, gases, and plants have been prepared for drinking, inhaling, and injecting. People have shown regrettable creativity in finding ways to dope themselves.

Our culture generally accepts the use of alcohol. Wine, for instance, has a venerable history, is associated even with sacred events, and is accompanied by certain "civilized" traditions: the tasting, the connoisseurship, and the tone of elevated refinement. To have a glass of wine with dinner is not frowned upon ... even three glasses ... where does one draw the line?

Beer and hard liquor also take part in the creation of images. The "real man," the two-fisted drinker who can "take on the whole house" — these stereotypes do influence people. But with the intake of any alcoholic beverage, a biological process takes over. Social use can develop over time into an addiction.

In addition to the various forms of alcohol, there are several kinds of drugs—legally prescribed medications, weight-loss compounds, and street drugs—used to alter consciousness. Even over-the-counter preparations such as aspirins, antacids, and laxatives have been misused.

An aura of glamour was originally attached to certain drugs newer to American mass culture, most notably cocaine. For some people, cocaine has an allure—they think it's exciting, special, an escape. Now we as a nation have begun to see cocaine and its derivatives such as crack, and other drugs, as the dangerous bombs they are.

Amphetamines in Weight Loss

Amphetamines (chemical compounds that speed up the nervous system) exist in many forms, some legal, some illegal. In earlier days legal, amphetamine-laced prescriptions to assist in weight loss were relatively easy to obtain. Weight-loss medications seemed like a godsend. They promised to suppress appetite—and for a short time, they could, but with unpleasant side effects: irritability, sleeplessness, and alteration of heart rate. For these reasons, physicians no longer prescribe amphetamines routinely for weight management. At best, they are a very short-term adjunct to more focused therapies, providing initial appetite control so that other, healthier techniques can be used.

A Family's Attitudes Toward Drug Use

A family's attitudes toward prescription and over-the-counter medicines may add a second layer of influence. Children who observe that parents consider a good stiff drink to be a cure for the day's troubles, or who hear adults casually refer to prescribed tranquilizers as routine necessities, are likely to assume that help can always be had from one substance or another. It is hard to learn self-sufficiency in such an environment. Teenagers in particular, ready to experiment with life and be accepted by peers, are vulnerable to media images, peer pressures, and adult role models.

Teens who use illegal, mind-altering drugs for fun or due to peer pressure will show behavior changes that include an aversion to food in some instances (for example, with the use of cocaine or amphetamines), or increased eating in others (for example, with the use of marijuana).

> *Alex was in trouble. He had been arrested for drunk driving and was now awaiting trial. At the time of the arrest, he was driving to the grocery store to get more food for an all-night binge. Because of his drinking, he was on probation at work, and this caused him to feel even more downhearted. He had recently tried cocaine and was thinking of using it again.*

When an eating problem is part of a larger constellation of substance use, sometimes it is simply circumstance that dictates which problem comes first to the attention of a friend, relative, or professional. The alcohol or other drug user may be seeing a therapist who does not have expertise in these areas. If so, the therapist may recommend that they continue working together while the patient consults another therapist specializing in substance abuse, or joins Alcoholics Anonymous or an alcohol and drug rehabilitation program. You may want to call A.A. or a local chemical dependency program for information. Many hospitals run (or host) such programs, or can refer you to agencies which do.

Are Eating Disorders Addictions?

Eating disorders can seem like addictions: the person feels out of control; her life is governed by the supply of a substance; she may try and fail to give up her habit. There may be secrecy, denial, and social isolation. Paying for her habit may cause her to deplete her bank account or even steal, draining energy from other areas of her life. Finally, as with alcohol and other drugs, the original sought-after effect changes: from being a solace and relief, food becomes a burden and a stressor. In recognition of these similarities, eating disordered people have sometimes been called "foodaholics."[2]

The addiction may appear as morning-till-night nibbling, rigid insistence on certain foods, or bingeing. As one writer noted,

> *The essential quality of an addiction is the feeling that there is never enough.* Bingers report constant cravings for food, but a binge never satisfies these cravings and, most important, indulging the urge to eat with a moderate amount of food is never enough.[3]

Another similarity is that in some families of alcoholics as well as in eating disorder sufferers, codependent behavior exists: as we saw in chapter seven, family members can unwittingly support the addictive pattern, for unconscious reasons of their own.

Eating disorders, however, are not exactly like alcoholism or drug abuse. First, no one can renounce food forever, so the "total abstinence" solution is unavailable to compulsive eaters.

This is very discouraging to some people with eating disorders—as well as to many dieters we know! But eating disorders *are* curable, though gaining the strength to eat sensibly can be more complex and stressful than simply "swearing off" a troublesome temptation.

You may have heard of *endorphins,* substances created by the brain that have been called "the body's natural opiates." These substances seem to be released by a variety of situations to create well-being or combat pain. They appear when a person is injured, when a person has been exercising strenuously, and when a person has just eaten. Thus, eating is generally experienced as a mild "high."

Somewhat more puzzling is the endorphin high reported by people who fast (do without food): the literature of mysticism tells stories of people who fast to gain special states of awareness. One expert feels that anorexics may be subtly attached to the state of semi-starvation through this endorphin high.[4] On the other side of the spectrum, bulimics can seem to be addicted to bingeing and even to the release purging offers.

Some people believe that sugar is addicting for them. They feel strong psychological cravings for sugar and find they do better in recovery when they abstain completely from it. While sugar certainly can cause harm when eaten in great quantities, it is not physiologically addicting. But it can be psychologically addicting. Some eating disorders treatment programs see sugar as an addictive drug, and the program is based on abstinence from it. We disagree with this approach. It seems to emphasize physiological aspects of addiction, to the neglect of the many psychological factors involved. Each person has a different relationship to sugar and other foods and must be evaluated individually. We have seen people recover beautifully and integrate sweets into their diets. We have also seen people from Twelve Step backgrounds who elect to abstain from sugar and recover very well.

The Multi-Substance Abuser

Some people abuse more than one substance. Such a person may drink and binge, use other drugs and binge, or do all three. For some, drug abuse is the more serious problem. For others, the eating disorder is primary, with alcohol a kind of entree to bingeing. The right order for dealing with the various substances depends on the individual. Some people feel more comfortable (and perhaps less embarrassed) approaching professionals for help with their eating disorder first. When alcoholism emerges in the course of treatment, they work with it then. Others are in more trouble with an alcohol or other drug problem and cannot afford to delay treatment for it.

You may wonder what to do if you suspect your loved one is addicted to a substance as well as having an eating problem. The combination may seem overwhelming and hopeless to try to overcome. Who could tackle several addictions and win? The solution is tackling one problem at a time. First, do your level best to get treatment started. Next, reflect a moment on your own habits. Do you knowingly or unwittingly encourage the person to think food, drugs, or alcohol can solve life's problems … that using them all the time is acceptable … that hangovers and missed workdays are amusing? If so, you can help your loved one by changing your viewpoint to create a healthier atmosphere. This could be an opportune time for you to contact a support group, talk to your doctor, drop in to a Twelve Step meeting (for example, Al-Anon or O-Anon), or call a therapist. Believe us, demonstrating a willingness to change your life can set a very powerful example!

Evaluating a Person for Treatment

A health care professional is really needed to assess the person you are concerned about and determine what needs to be tackled first. The clinician will try to determine which addiction creates the most immediately dangerous consequences. A bottle-a-day whiskey habit is obviously more dangerous than an eating disorder if the person has blackouts or continues to drive when drunk. It should be addressed first.

Hannah was eighteen. She came in with her mother to consult a therapist about a suspected eating disorder. Hannah revealed that she also regularly smoked marijuana, and twice after all-night parties didn't remember how she got home. She was sexually active, but erratic in taking precautions against pregnancy, and wholly reckless in protecting against sexually transmitted diseases.

The risks she was running were obvious to the therapist, who questioned her more fully about her drinking and other behaviors. A picture emerged of someone who was almost suicidal in her actions — drunk driving, risking disease, accepting drugs from strangers, minimizing others' concern. For instance, once she was so drunk her friends took her home, but she insisted on trying to go out again.

With this in perspective, the therapist recommended Hannah begin an intensive chemical dependency program. He promised that he would work with her on her eating disorder as soon as the more dangerous substance-use problems were managed.

The professional conducting the evaluation will ask such questions as these:

- Is the person's substance use reactive (in response to a specific crisis or disappointment), or a coping strategy used continually?
- Are there immediate dangers?
- Are there multiple dependencies?
- Does the person admit the problem or try to minimize it?
- Does she have an adequate support system, or is she isolated?
- What is the risk of suicide?

In Hannah's case, it seemed that various substances were her habitual crutch, and in an indirect way, she expressed suicidal despair. Favorable signs were Hannah's willingness to consult a therapist, and her mother's concern.

Convincing a person that she is at risk and should get help can be a delicate task. Conveying both the danger and the hope, without frightening her away from treatment, takes tact and perseverance. One concerned family member confronted her sister and set limits: "Sarah, I'm worried about your drinking. It's no longer a joke. I don't feel right having you drive my car at this point, or picking up the kids from child care. I'm going to ask you to see a counselor and to join A.A."

Many programs and therapists require an alcoholic or other drug abuser to get help from a Twelve Step program or other self-help program to supplement individual therapy. For someone with a serious dependency, one hour of treatment a week, or even two hours, is not enough! Further, many therapists— and we are among them—expect the client to come to sessions substance-free, believing that if chemical dependency is not addressed in the early stages of therapy, further progress is sabotaged.

Once the evaluation is completed, several avenues exist. Some people need inpatient help before they can be helped as outpatients. They must detoxify and be in control of their cravings enough to be helped by an outpatient therapist. Others can be helped as outpatients, and their recovery from substance abuse proceeds along with their recovery from the eating disorder.

The Script and Its Players: "Significant Others"

Many years ago, a clever psychologist named Steven Karpman noticed something strange about the "significant others" in the lives of his drinking patients. They seemed to fall into types, and together with the patient they formed a kind of script, made up of the Rescuer, the Persecutor, and the Victim. This is the Karpman triangle. The alcoholic in this play is the *Victim*. The *Persecutor* is anyone — especially a wife or husband—who criticizes the Victim's drinking. The *Rescuer* may be a drinking friend who shares (or at least listens to) the Victim's complaints on how tough life is. The Rescuer's timely interruptions of the Persecutor's criticism make it easy for the Victim to continue drinking.

We have noticed a similar array of characters in the lives of people with eating disorders. The *Critic* is always ready to find fault. The *Envied One* might be an attractive model, a successful fellow student, or a career ideal. The *One Who Needs Help* may be the depressed friend who needs a shoulder to cry on, or it may be the overworked waitress, or even the hungry children in Africa. She herself is the *Victim-Heroine*, who could further be characterized as the *Repentant Sinner*, the *Caretaker*, or *World Savior*.

These stereotypes, however, exist mostly in the mind and memory of the eating disordered person. She sees the world in these terms, and tends to notice people who fit the familiar "slots" in her script. This means that her life is full of people to placate, people to envy, and people to take care of.

Families and the Problems They Share

Other family members may have problems with alcohol or other drugs and the eating disordered person may pick up the habit from them. Or she may worry about their substance abuse in addition to her other worries, or keep her life in disarray as an act of loyalty to them. This problem may be difficult to solve even when she has entered a hospital treatment program.

Researchers often find substance abuse in the family backgrounds of eating disorder patients. You may have heard of the "adult children of alcoholics" syndrome. This is a cluster of personality and behavior traits often found in people who grew up in a family with one (or both) parents drinking out of control. These traits include caretaking, perfectionism, low self-esteem, isolation, and suppressing one's emotions. Does this sound familiar? It is very similar to the personality of some eating disordered persons!

Relapses

Your eating disordered friend or relative has almost certainly made many attempts to regain control over her food and eating. Sometimes she may have succeeded for weeks or even months. But then a slip occurred, and she seemed to go "back to square one." She may even conclude that she will never recover, or that she is a bad person. Knowing the difference between a lapse and a relapse may help you offer support in times of difficulty.

Researchers distinguish a *lapse,* or single slip, from *relapse,* which is a longer-lasting state of lost control. When a person trying to give up a habit fails and loses control, this violation of self-imposed rules can cause even greater loss of control.[5] The lapsers then blame themselves and conclude, "I'm no good," or "I'll never succeed." Researchers have found almost the same results among people with eating disorders, who express beliefs such as these:

- "My binge has spoiled all my progress to date—now I must start over."
- "My binge this afternoon is evidence that I fail at everything."
- "Since I could not stop a binge today, I will never be able to recover."[6]

The *belief* is more damaging than the slip. So, as experts are finding, the lapser's best next step is forgiving herself and realizing that this error is not the end of the world. One thing a therapist can do is ask the eating disordered person to divide her day into two-hour segments. If she slips at 1:00 P.M., she has messed up only one time slot, not the entire day.

Alcohol and other drug use complicate the picture for an eating disordered person. The friend or family can help by not colluding in denial, by encouraging recovery, and by setting reasonable limits.

Suicidal Feelings and Self-Harm

Without wishing to alarm you, we should discuss the possibility that your loved one may feel so bad about herself and life that she is ready to give up. For some people, this is nothing more than a feeling that comes and goes, sometimes more strongly than at other times.

For others, depression is so deep, or repeated failures to recover have sapped vitality so much that death seems preferable. Some of these people make suicide attempts. One study compared ninety-five patients with anorexia nervosa, bulimia, and bingeing anorexia to see the tendency of depression and attempted suicide.[7] Researchers found that 80 percent were depressed, and that 20 percent of these people had attempted suicide. Events that led to the suicide attempts were broken relationships, fights, loss of control over food, and feeling low and hopeless. The authors of one study of bingeing anorexics reported significant incidences of stealing, alcohol or other drug use, self-mutilation, and suicide attempts.[8]

What should you do? First, remember that you must do whatever is necessary to keep your friend alive. If she talks about suicide, you should notify her doctor or therapist at once. If you see her with a knife or gun in hand, call the emergency number (911) and have her taken to a safe place (usually a local hospital). A person who has thought about when and how to end life is more likely to make a suicide attempt, so try to find out if she has a plan. Even if you are not sure, pass on to the therapist any information you have about suicidal thoughts or statements.

Other kinds of self-harm can be more subtle.

- She may cut or burn herself in places usually covered by clothes.
- She may pull out her hair, or cut it herself in an angry and destructive way.
- She may go outside without a jacket in midwinter, secretly hoping to become ill.
- She may deprive herself of medicine when ill or of comforts such as warm blankets.

If you notice such self-harming behaviors, tell her what you see and how it makes you feel. ("I feel frightened and upset when I see you cutting yourself.") If you believe her health is in danger, bring her to an emergency room or insist she see her doctor. You don't have to play dumb—but neither can you force her to get help if she is not in physical danger. If she is your minor child and is endangering her health, you must get her prompt medical attention. Her therapist can work with her on reducing and eliminating her self-harming behaviors.

Sexual Abuse

More commonly than a civilized society would like to admit, girls and women are exposed to the possibility of sexual attack. Research has shown that victims of molestation or rape may experience a variety of posttraumatic symptoms, including disordered eating. Rarer, but also occurring, is sexual abuse of males.

Molestation is a dreadful invasion of a child's body, which also violates her trust (since the offender is often someone known to her and may accompany the act with threats), and her self-esteem (since she was unable to protect herself and may now believe she is a no-good person).

A similar loss of power and self-esteem affect the adult victim. Food becomes a consolation, a mode of further self-punishment, and a protection: the fat body is somehow felt to be a safeguard against further attack.

Not every sexual abuse victim develops an eating disorder, and not every eating disordered person was sexually abused, but it happens often enough that it just might be a hidden factor for the person you care about. But do not take it upon yourself to interrogate her or demand she do something about it. This trauma is usually a person's deepest secret, one she may not be ready to reveal even to her therapist. Sooner or later, we hope she will do so, for no matter how long ago the event occurred, there is great therapeutic value in expressing the legitimate rage and in reclaiming a sense of body esteem and trust.

Conclusion

In this chapter we have discussed some pretty alarming subjects—stealing, substance abuse, suicide, and sexual abuse. We feel it's important for you to know all the possible factors that may interact in the lives of eating disorder patients. But this does not mean that your loved one must *necessarily* have any of these problems in addition to her eating disorder. Many (maybe even most) people struggling with their eating behaviors do not have such traumas, but merely sensitive personalities, coupled with a desire to please and an unfortunate practice of diverting emotions into a preoccupation with food and physiques.

In practical terms, you can be on the alert to these facts of life, ready to step in if your loved one is over her head in multiple problems — but don't panic and automatically assume the worst.

CHAPTER 16

Some Final Thoughts

A Word to Parents

Laura, Kristie's mother (whom we met in chapter thirteen), found that one of the most difficult things for her to deal with was her guilt and self-blame. She kept feeling that if only she had done something differently ten years ago, five years ago, yesterday, none of this would have happened. Many parents feel this way. Remember, eating disorders have many causes. Furthermore, even when we look at possible family causes, we do not use concepts of villain and victim. A family is more like a complex game or dance, with its own unique patterns. Some patterns lead to desirable outcomes, others to less desirable ones. Changing destructive patterns can be initiated by any member and is easiest when all members are committed to positive change.

Some areas within a family repeatedly come to the attention of therapists.

- The distribution of *power* may seem unbalanced: one parent may be treated as a nonentity while one child (who may be the patient) is treated as an adult before she is ready.
- A child may become a *go-between*, a message-bearer or unofficial therapist to the family, long before she has the resources to handle such a difficult task.
- There may be *alliances* that cast the family into opposing camps.

167

- The family may have an emotional style of *communication* that leaves feelings unstated or unattended to. This makes it difficult for members to discuss important issues, and misunderstandings may arise.
- Another problem we see often is *conflict avoidance,* a style in which areas of disagreement are swept under the rug.

Having one or more of these characteristics does not mean a given family is "sick." All families have difficulties in living together, rearing and then letting go of children, and managing work and play. The point is not to blame yourself, but to learn and move on. By reading this book, you're showing you care and are willing to explore change.

You may be invited to participate in family therapy sessions. Unexplored family conflict may emerge. A visible symptom such as the eating disorder is like a flashing light on a car's dashboard, indicating that something is amiss. Airing the problem, while temporarily embarrassing or painful, can be a first step leading the patient back to health, and often also benefits other family members. We want to emphasize that all feelings are real, and deserve a family's respectful attention.

A Word to Partners

Partners, like parents, worry. They may blame themselves and try to help as best they can. At times they struggle to realize that their mate is not their child, and that while they can suggest or arrange treatment, they cannot force another adult into it. It is best to acknowledge the eating problem. But don't focus on it to the exclusion of other problems or strengths in the eating disordered person and the relationship.

If a partner is overly concerned about the problem and places undue emphasis on the body, he or she may be obscuring other issues by the attitude, *If only she didn't have this eating problem everything would be fine.* We have seen some couples hide myriad problems behind "her eating disorder."

Sex and appearance are closely linked in our society. For many women and men (not just those with eating disorders) sex is an activity fraught with embarrassment because it involves revealing the body. Others find it hard to believe that someone would like their body when they themselves judge it as ugly.

Some people with eating disorders hate their bodies, feel ugly, doubt anyone finds them attractive, and recoil from the thought of surrendering to what they consider uncontrollable urges. Is it any wonder that sex is not desirable to many of them? Some others seem to "binge" on sex, and to have unrewarding contacts that only reinforce their self-rejection. Still others have quite satisfactory sexual relationships and enjoy their bodies.

If you are in a relationship with an eating disordered person, it is reassuring to know that when the eating disorder is resolved, sensual pleasure and intimacy may be restored. Professional help is also available. Sex therapy, a form of psychotherapy offered by licensed mental health practitioners, uses tested behavioral and psychological techniques that have helped many people.

Please note that anorexic women can become pregnant even though their menstrual cycle has not resumed. Thus, couples should use birth control unless they are trying to conceive. Be aware, however, that if a bulimic is vomiting, birth control pills may be lost and are thus unreliable.

A spouse's anger and frustration at living with an eating disordered person can be intense. You can share these feelings in a nonblaming way: "I get so frustrated when I realize you've been in therapy for a while and you're still bingeing. It's hard for me to watch you struggle with your problem." You don't need to protect your partner from your reality, but respect her as you share your thoughts and feelings.

Perhaps you feel you are reaching your limit in being with your eating disordered partner. This is important to share also.

For some partners, couple therapy helps them ride out the eating disorder.

A Word to Brothers and Sisters

Do you worry about your sibling, or feel left out because he or she seems to get all the attention? We want you to know that your observations and needs are important too. Perhaps you have valuable clues about the eating disordered person's habits. Perhaps the topsy-turvy patterns that cause (or reflect) eating disorders are making you unhappy, and you can shed light on these patterns and their effects.

It may be that, along with other meanings, a bulimic habit contains a message to you.[1] Often, the bulimic is trying to help her brothers and sisters with the message behind the disorder:

- *I'll bring us together.*
- *See, I too have a problem.*
- *I will protect you (by deflecting attention).*
- *I will make you important.*

Or the message may be aimed at getting parents' attention, or the attention of others through winning weight-loss competitions. Uncovering such unspoken communications and working to make them unnecessary can help the eating disordered person recover. We predict that this will benefit you too.

A Word to Friends

A friend cannot make another adult (or teenager) go for help, but you can suggest, encourage, and be a steady "other" who can define limits and keep them. Your friendship can focus on shared interests that do not involve food, eating, or weight. She is more than an eating problem, and your relationship is greater than one topic.

Friends can listen and help the person with an eating disorder express her feelings. They can provide caring and support, reminding the person that she is valued. If you find all your friendship time is spent listening to her talk about her problem, you may want to ask for a more balanced relationship.

Be aware of her need for privacy about her problem. It is crucial that you not talk to others about it: if she has confided in you, she has trusted you not to relate the news to other people.

Be sensitive when you are in public together, such as in restaurants. It is her business what she orders and eats. This is especially important if you, too, have a food or eating conflict. Her path to recovery is as legitimate as yours, even if the paths are different. People use therapy, Overeaters Anonymous (O.A.), reading, thinking, and other methods to recover and grow. Mutual respect will help keep your friendship healthy.

A Word to the Patient: How to Help Your Family and Friends Help You

Many of our patients have struggled to redefine their relationships as they work on eating conflicts. For example, Amy wanted her husband to support her in her move toward health, but didn't want him to tell her what to eat. He was so worried that he tended to hover over her like a mother hen. Meanwhile, Jeffrey faced a similar problem, since every week his wife asked him about his progress in therapy and he felt scrutinized. Both Amy and Jeffrey needed to create the optimum balance of concern, and independence, in their relationships. We suggest our adult patients do the following to help others help them:

1. Remind your friend or family member, "Everybody needs support, but nobody needs a food guard." Explain that it is counterproductive for him or her to peer at your plate, analyzing your meal and your ability to eat and digest it. Except in a hospital or specialized program, for one person to monitor another's food consumption may make the eating disordered person feel like an infant. Although there have been exceptions with couples, we have found it better for the concerned other

to offer fuzzy general support which conveys the message, *I love and care about you. I trust that you will move toward health.*

2. Remind your friend that the same applies to exercise. Nobody needs an exercise guard either.

3. It is all right to choose areas to work on first, while delegating other areas for later attention.

4. Not every friend or family member has to be informed in detail about your eating problem and its treatment. Unless your problem is endangering your life or health, you get to decide who knows what, and when.

> *Kate's tendency to let other people tell her what to think and feel was at the root of her problem. Her therapist coached Kate in discovering her own opinion, expressing it, and defending it. Together, they imagined how various people in Kate's life would react once she began to speak up for herself. These "rehearsals" enabled Kate to learn that her thoughts and feelings were valuable. She learned that her mother wouldn't die of horror if Kate expressed her ideas, and that being assertive is not the same as being a tyrant. These discoveries paved the way for Kate to reevaluate her relationship to her body and how it looked to others.*
>
> *Kate was now nearly done with formal therapy, though she realized learning about oneself is a never-ending process. At her next-to-last session, Andrea asked her what message she would like to pass on to other people just beginning to tackle an eating disorder.*
>
> *"I'll tell you," Kate replied. "The most important thing is,* everything you learn is part of the cure, *no matter how small it may seem at the time. It made a big difference to me when I learned to say 'no' to people who wanted me to do favors for them. It sounds a little corny, but you have to love and forgive yourself even if cure seems a thousand miles away. Hating yourself hasn't worked yet—so give love a try!" Here she chuckled as she remembered how she used to rely on self-hate in order to motivate herself.*

"I don't binge and purge anymore. When I'm sad, I cry. When I'm proud of myself, I enjoy it. Sometimes I want to be with people; sometimes I want to be alone. I never knew that both are okay! I thought there was some rule about how to be. Actually," she added thoughtfully, *"there is a rule—learn to trust yourself!"*

Prevention

Clearly, the best way to reduce the tremendous toll that eating disorders — or any illnesses—take on people is to prevent them from happening in the first place.

Experts are virtually unanimous in agreeing that cultural influences play a significant part in eating disorders. Particularly blamed is the fashionable thin image. What a concerned friend or relative can do is to introduce more healthy influences. Praise and reward your loved ones for reasons other than appearance. Reduce comments you make about appearances of other people. Support school and community efforts to teach kids to look beyond the "thin is beautiful" mentality. If we are parents, we should question the wisdom of children dieting, and help our kids cultivate a love of healthful and fun foods, movement and exercise, and friendship and life.

Knowledge about eating disorders may help. Many of our patients have said, "I'm calling you because I'm worried about harming my body." They had heard of medical risks, and this information helped them take the necessary step to recovery. Though on a national scale knowledge is slow to translate into action, preventive health care campaigns in this country have gradually had an impact on exercise, on safe sex practices, and on quitting smoking. We hope the same will be true for eating disorders.

Should You be Optimistic or Pessimistic?

What are the prospects for your eating disordered friend or relative's recovery? You may have heard dire warnings about how difficult recovery can be, or you may have heard of miracle cures. You may have been through a long struggle already that left you weary and discouraged. What do the experts think of a patient's chances?

While many experts respect the difficulty of recovering from eating disorders, it is clear that progress is being made in the field. Research on diagnosis, treatment, and basic biology is being carried out at a phenomenal rate. Associations, conferences, and journals dedicated to eating disorders have been established, and through them knowledge is being shared very quickly. Collaboration among experts is common, so that a patient is less and less likely to be funneled into one narrow approach to treatment. As a field, we are working on discriminating among different kinds of bulimics and anorexics and compulsive eaters, so that we will know exactly which patient is most likely to benefit from medications, which from psychotherapy, and which from hospitalization or other forms of treatment.

Many people with eating disorders have made full recoveries. Many others have made such substantial progress that they can resume a normal life. So, though we encourage you to take the eating disorder seriously, we also wish to extend hope.

A Final Word

We know that any one book cannot begin to answer all the questions a person may have about his or her loved one's eating disorder. We hope we have made a start by describing issues and solutions that we have found important in our practices.

While we recognize that change is not easy, we believe that most people deeply wish to resolve their eating disorders, and when the time is right, they are willing to work hard to do so. We hope that your journey with your loved one will be a fruitful and illuminating one.

Endnotes

CHAPTER 2: NOT MY DAUGHTER!

1. Hilde Bruch, Developmental considerations of anorexia nervosa and obesity. *Canadian Journal of Psychiatry,* 1981, 26 (4), 212-217.

CHAPTER 3: A GLIMPSE INTO ANOTHER WORLD

1. Susan C. Wooley and O. Wayne Wooley, Intensive outpatient and residential treatment for bulimia. In D. M. Garner and P. E. Garfinkel (Eds.). *Handbook of Psychotherapy for Anorexia Nervosa and Bulimia.* New York: Guilford Press, 1985, 400.

CHAPTER 4: WAYS EATING GOES WRONG

1. Judith S. Lazerson, Voices of bulimia: experiences in integrated psychotherapy. *Psychotherapy: Theory, Research and Practice,* 1984, 21 (4), 504.
2. Geneen Roth, *Feeding the Hungry Heart: The Experience of Compulsive Eating.* New York: New American Library Signet, 1982, 15-16.
3. Avis Rumney, *Dying to Please: Anorexia Nervosa and Its Cure.* Jefferson, N. C.: McFarland & Co., 1983, 16
4. Roth, *Feeding the Hungry Heart,* 37.
5. Poem is by Sheila M. Bramson, quoted in *Pathology of Eating: Psychology and Treatment,* by Sara Gilbert. London: Routledge and Kegan Paul, 1986, 92-93. Reprinted with permission of Sheila M. Bramson.

CHAPTER 5: WHAT CAUSES EATING DISORDERS?

1. Susan C. Wooley and O. Wayne Wooley, Should obesity be treated at all? In A. J. Stunkard and E. Stellar (Eds.), *Eating and Its Disorders.* New York: Raven, 1984.

2. Jack Katz, Some reflections on the nature of the eating disorders: On the need for humility. *International Journal of Eating Disorders,* 1985, 4 (4A), 622.
3. Ancel Keys, J. Brozek, A. Henschel, O. Mickelsen, and H. L. Taylor, *The Biology of Human Starvation.* Minneapolis: University of Minnesota Press, 1950.
4. David M. Garner, Cognitive therapy for anorexia nervosa. In Kelly D. Brownell and J. P. Foreyt (Eds.), *Handbook of Eating Disorders: Physiology, Psychology and Treatment of Obesity, Anorexia and Bulimia.* New York: Basic Books, Inc., 1986, 307.
5. W. Bennett and J. Gurin, *The Dieter's Dilemma.* New York: Basic Books, Inc., 1982.
6. Janet Polivy and C. Peter Herman, Dieting and bingeing: A causal analysis. *American Psychologist,* 1985, 40 (2), 200.
7. J. Hubert Lacey, Sian Coker, and S. A. Birtchnell, Bulimia: Factors associated with its etiology and maintenance. *International Journal of Eating Disorders, 1986.* 5 (3), 475-487.

CHAPTER 7: HELPING THE EATING DISORDERED PERSON BEGIN TREATMENT

1. Barbara P. Kinoy, Self-help groups in the management of anorexia nervosa and bulimia: A theoretical base. *Transactional Analysis Journal,* 1985, 15 (1), 73-78.

CHAPTER 10: YOU AND YOUR NEEDS

1. Jack Vognsen, Brief, strategic treatment of bulimia. *Transactional Analysis Journal,* 1985, 15 (1), 79-84. 80.

CHAPTER 11: COMMUNICATING YOUR FEELINGS

1. This chapter is based substantially on Linda Riebel, Communication skills for eating disordered clients, *Psychotherapy: Theory, Research, Practice, Training,* 1989, 26 (1), 69-74.

CHAPTER 13: SPECIAL GROUPS—CHILDREN

1. Ellyn Satter, *How to Get Your Kid to Eat—But Not Too Much,* Palo Alto, Calif.: Bull Publishing, 1987.
2. Write to SHAPEDOWN, 11 Library Place, San Anselmo, CA 94960 for the program nearest you. For information about practitioners trained to manage adolescent obesity, contact The Center for Adolescent Obesity, Box 900, Department of Family Community Medicine, University of California at San Francisco, San Francisco, CA 94143.

CHAPTER 14: SPECIAL GROUPS—MEN AND BOYS

1. Arnold E. Anderson, Males with eating disorders. In Felix E. F. Larocca (Ed.), *Eating Disorders.* London: Jossey-Bass, 1986.
2. John A. Schneider, and W. Steward Agras, Bulimia in males: a matched comparison with females. *International Journal of Eating Disorders,* 1987, 6 (2), 235-252.
3. Anderson, Males with eating disorders.
4. Michelle Cameron and Michael Charles, Eating behavior of male racing jockeys. Unpublished manuscript written in 1987.

CHAPTER 15: THERE MAY BE OTHER PROBLEMS

1. A. B. Heilbrun and D. L. Bloomfield, Cognitive differences between bulimic and anorexic females: self-control deficits in bulimics. *International Journal of Eating Disorders* 1986, 5 (2), 109-222. See also P. E. Garfinkel and D. M. Garner, Bulimia in anorexia nervosa. In R. C. Hawkins, W. J. Fremouw, P. F. Clement (Eds.), *The Binge-Purge Syndrome: Diagnosis, Treatment and Research,* New York: Springer, 1984. See also S. Gilbert, *Pathology of Eating: Psychology and Treatment,* London: Routledge and Kegan Paul, 1986. Also R. L. Pyle, J. E. Mitchell, and E. E. Eckert, Bulimia: A report of 34 cases. *Journal of Clinical Psychiatry 1981,* 42 (2), 60-64.

2. Sandra G. Stoltz, Beware of boundary issues. *Transactional Analysis Journal*, 1985, 15 (1), 37-41.
3. J. Gormally, The obese binge eater: diagnosis, etiology and clinical issues. In R. C. Hawkins, W. J. Fremouw, and P. F. Clement (Eds.), *The Binge-Purge Syndrome: Diagnosis, Treatment and Research.* New York: Springer, 1984, 51.
4. G. I. Szmukler, Some comments on the link between anorexia nervosa and affective disorder. *International Journal of Eating Disorders*, 1987, 6 (2), 181-189.
5. Kelly D. Brownell, A. G. Marlatt, E. Lichtenstein, and G. T. Wilson, Understanding and preventing relapse. *American Psychologist*, 1986, 41 (7), 765-782.
6. David M. Garner, Wendi Rockert, Marion P. Olmsted, Craig Johnson, and Donald V. Coscina, Psychoeducational principles in the treatment of bulimia and anorexia nervosa. In David M. Garner and P. E. Garfinkel (Eds.), *Handbook of Psychotherapy for Anorexia Nervosa and Bulimia.* New York: Guilford, 1985, 554.
7. James E. Mitchell and R. L. Pyle, Characteristics of bulimia. In J. E. Mitchell (Ed.), *Anorexia and Bulimia: Diagnosis and Treatment.* Minneapolis: University of Minnesota Press, 1985. See also S. Nevo, Bulimic symptoms: Prevalence and ethnic differences among college women. *International Journal of Eating Disorders*, 1985, 4 (2), 151-168. Also D. A. Thompson, K. M. Berg, and L. A. Shatford, The heterogeneity of bulimic symptomatology: Cognitive and behavioral dimensions. *International Journal of Eating Disorders* 1985, 6 (2), 215-234. Also D. E. Schotte and A. J. Stunkard, Bulimia versus bulimic behaviors on a college campus. *Journal of the American Medical Association*, 1987, 258 (9), 1213-1215. Also E. J. Button and A. Whitehouse, Subclinical anorexia nervosa. *Psychological Medicine*, 1981, 11, 509-516.
8. Paul E. Garfinkel and David M. Garner, Bulimia in anorexia nervosa. In R. C. Hawkins, W. J. Fremouw, P. C. Clement (Eds.), *The Binge-Purge Syndrome: Diagnosis, Treatment and Research.* New York: Springer, 1984.

CHAPTER 16: SOME FINAL THOUGHTS

1. Karen Gail Lewis, Bulimia as a communication to siblings. *Psychotherapy: Theory, Research, Practice, Training.* 1987, 24 (3S), 640-645.

Suggested Reading

The following books may help you understand your significant other's problem and the different forms of treatment now in use. They represent differing viewpoints. Keep in mind that the authors are reporting to the best of their ability the traits of the people they have worked with and the techniques that worked best for them. Your friend may not fit the description you find in a given book.

Concerned friends and relatives sometimes misinterpret statistics, or recall a particularly vivid case example and become unnecessarily upset. If in your reading you encounter anything that alarms you, please investigate further.

Bennett, W. and J. Gurin (1982). *The Dieter's Dilemma.* New York: Basic Books, Inc. A very well-written summary of the research documenting the set-point theory, which is now well accepted in the field.

Boskind-White, Marlene and William C. White, Jr., (1983). *Bulimarexia: The Binge-Purge Cycle.* New York: W.W. Norton & Co., Inc. A responsible survey of what we know about bulimia, its causes and treatments.

Bruch, Hilde (1978). *The Golden Cage: The Enigma of Anorexia Nervosa.* Cambridge, Mass.: Harvard University Press. A classic, easy-to-read book on the world of the anorexic.

Chernin, Kim (1981). *The Obsession: Reflections on the Tyranny of Slenderness.* New York: Harper Colophon. A fine synthesis of philosophy, social commentary, and psychology, this book examines our fixation on the slender body, and what it means to the individual and the culture.

Hollis, Judi (1985). *Fat Is a Family Affair.* Center City, Minn.: Hazelden Educational Materials. A moving discussion of eating disorders and the family's involvement. The book describes how people can become eating disorder sufferers, and how the person, and the family, can begin recovery.

Hall, Lindsey and Leigh Cohn (Eds.). (1987). *Recoveries: True Stories by People Who Conquered Addictions and Compulsions.* Carlsbad, Calif.: Gurze Books. This anthology collects the accounts of people recovering from alcoholism, other drug abuse, bulimia, anorexia, and suicidal impulses.

Matsakis, Aphrodite (1987). *Please Don't Give Me Chocolates.* Center City, Minn.: Hazelden Educational Materials. This pamphlet addresses the feelings concerned others of recovering compulsive overeaters have.

Migliore, Joanna (1987). *Twelve Steps for Parents.* Center City, Minn.: Hazelden Educational Materials. This pamphlet discusses common problems such as humiliation, shaken self-worth, and lack of trust that parents of children with eating disorders may suffer.

Millman, Marcia (1980). *Such a Pretty Face: Being Fat in America.* New York: W.W. Norton & Co., Inc. This book provides a graphic tour of life for the fat person. Included are chapters on O.A., children, fat camps, the desexualization of fat the antisocial image of fat people, and recent efforts to build esteem.

Orbach, Susie (1978). *Fat is a Feminist Issue: The Anti-Diet Guide to Permanent Weight Loss.* New York: Berkley. A classic many people have already read. The main thesis is that overeating and excess weight are natural responses to untenable social conditions.

Polivy Janet and C.P. Herman (1983). *Breaking the Diet Habit: The Natural Weight Alternative.* New York: Basic Books, Inc. The authors, respected researchers in the biology of dieting, explain the dangers of restrained eating, why the body resists weight loss, and the relationship of dieting to eating disorders.

Riebel, Linda K. (1988). *Understanding Eating Disorders: A Guide for Healthcare Professionals.* Sacramento, Calif.: Robert D. Anderson Publishing Co. An informative, unbiased survey of the many theories of cause and treatment, drawn from recent research and clinical experience. A concise practical handbook for professionals (nurses, teachers, counselors) who may encounter eating disorders among their clientele.

Roth, Geneen (1982). *Feeding the Hungry Heart: The Experience of Compulsive Eating.* New York: New American Library Signet. Not for the squeamish, this book catalogues in graphic detail the world of the bulimic, but is useful in letting patients know they are understood and are not alone.

Roth, Geneen (1984). *Breaking Free from Compulsive Eating.* Indianapolis: Bobbs Merrill. A more practical guide to recovery, including the author's personal experience.

Rumney, Avis (1983). *Dying to Please: Anorexia Nervosa and Its Cure.* Jefferson, N. C.: McFarland & Co. The author, a therapist and recovered anorexic, combines a personal account with a step-by-step explanation of several forms of therapy, complete with the relevant research.

Additional books on alcoholism, the adult children of alcoholics syndrome, overeating, and other topics can be obtained from Hazelden Educational Materials or at meetings of Twelve Step groups.

Index

A

Acute abdominal pain, 55

Addiction theory of eating disorders, 157-58

Adolescents, eating behavior and disorder development in, 141-44

"Adult children of alcoholics" syndrome, 162

Aftercare, hospital, 98-99

Alcohol abuse, and eating disorders, 155-57

Alcoholics Anonymous, 66, 157

American Anorexia/Bulimia Association, 66

Amphetamines, in weight loss, 155-56

Anger, repression of, 20

Anorexia nervosa, definition of, 32

Anorexic patterns, 32-33

Anorexics: distorted body image of, 32, 129; general signs of eating disorders in, 59; hospitalization for, 91; importance of control among, 32-33; medical problems in, 51-53; perfectionism of, 22

Antidepressants, 72

Art therapy, 75

Assertiveness, lack of, 20-21

B

Binge, definition of, 29

Bingeing, medical problems caused by, 52

Blood chemistry imbalance, 54

Body, what to say about the, 129-30

Body-esteem development, 139-41

Body image conflict, 21

Body image and esteem therapy, 76

Bruch, Hilde, 15

Bulimia, definition of, 31

Bulimic patterns, 31

Other titles that will interest you . . .

Fat Is a Family Affair
by Judi Hollis, Ph.D.

A unique and moving discussion of eating disorders and the family's involvement. This book deals with how a person becomes an eating disorder sufferer and describes how the person, and the family, can begin recovery. 180 pp.
Order No. 1091

Twelve Steps for Parents
by Joanna Migliore

This pamphlet discusses the common problems—such as humiliation, shaken self-worth, and lack of trust—parents of a child with an eating disorder may encounter. 20 pp.
Order No. 5555

Please Don't Give Me Chocolates
by Aphrodite Matsakis, Ph.D.

Addressed in this pamphlet are the common feelings experienced by concerned others of recovering overeaters. Personal stories convey how your acceptance of their eating disorder and recovery program can help a loved one. 32 pp.
Order No. 5406
